D1594302

AMERICA'S URBAN CRISIS AND THE ADVENT OF COLOR-BLIND POLITICS

AMERICA'S URBAN
CRISIS
AND THE
ADVENT
OF COLOR-BLIND
POLITICS

EDUCATION, INCARCERATION, SEGREGATION,
AND THE FUTURE OF U.S. MULTIRACIAL DEMOCRACY

EDITED BY
CURTIS L. IVERY AND JOSHUA A. BASSETT

ROWMAN & LITTLEFIELD PUBLISHERS, INC.
Lanham • Boulder • New York • Toronto • Plymouth, UK

Published by Rowman & Littlefield Publishers, Inc.
A wholly owned subsidiary of The Rowman & Littlefield Publishing Group, Inc.
4501 Forbes Boulevard, Suite 200, Lanham, Maryland 20706
http://www.rowmanlittlefield.com

Estover Road, Plymouth PL6 7PY, United Kingdom

British Library Cataloguing in Publication Information Available

Library of Congress Cataloging-in-Publication Data

America's Urban Crisis and the Advent of Color-blind Politics:
Education, incarceration, segregation, and the future of U.S. multiracial democracy / edited by Curtis L. Ivery & Joshua A. Bassett.
 p. cm.
 ISBN 978-1-4422-1099-8 (cloth : alk. paper) — ISBN 978-1-4422-1101-8 (ebook)
 1. Educational equalization. 2. Discrimination in education. 3. Imprisonment. I. Ivery, Curtis L. II. Bassett, Joshua A.
 LC213.E377 2011
 379.2'6—dc22   2011012984

CONTENTS

ACKNOWLEDGMENTS

For all the wealth and intelligence we have in this country, we remain in a crisis—educationally, economically, socially, racially, and emotionally. Yet, there are those who, quite simply, remain committed to making a difference.

It is my hope that this book has an impact on the lives of those who read it and those they encounter. Knowledge has a domino effect and affects so many and in various ways. It is also my hope that we as a race, a people, a culture, and a country continue to move toward becoming the society that America was promised to be.

America—the promise of freedom and equal opportunity; the potential of education for all. For our children, these remain promises and possibilities that we must help them realize.

To this effort, I must thank those who generously contributed their time, talents, and wealth of knowledge, experiences, perspectives, and opinions. The various backgrounds of our contributors prove that there are no real barriers for those who believe in the power of partnerships.

To the scholars who have helped make this book a true and valued resource, I thank you. To those who continue to support my efforts and the efforts of others who work toward a better community, I thank you. I also want to give special thanks to my good friend Dr. Cornel West, who offered invaluable inspiration and support to this project.

For your willingness to explore the depths of discussion in this book, I thank you, the reader. Your belief in and celebration of the written word speak volumes about the potential we all hold for a higher calling, for ourselves and each other.

Most important, I thank my loving wife, Ola, and our children, Marcus and Angela. Of all the things that matter, my family is the most important. They have taught me to love, to live, to learn, and to give. Those are the principles of my life. Without my family, I would not be who I am or be able to do what I love.

For all of these things, I give thanks.

Curtis L. Ivery
Detroit, 2011

Each of us experiences our own life as a result of the contributions of those who preceded us in a generational responsibility that seeks to continuously improve the human condition.

This is a collective work by many whose lives reflect that generational responsibility. They share a hope, belief, and trust that understanding where we have been will help all of us better understand where we are in order to build a better future.

America's urban communities have always been a foundation for our present and a leading gateway to our future. Where we are now is a critical moment in our history to consider the past, present, and promise of urban America, and the urban crisis before us.

This work is dedicated in appreciation to all who have given to me and inspired me to pick up and carry the torch and hopefully cultivate and motivate another generation to keep the flame of hope and promise alive.

This would never have happened without the countless people who have helped me along in my life, from neighbors and teachers to students and inspirational leaders.

I especially wish to acknowledge and thank my wife, Michelle, for her intellectual challenges and guidance to my work while extending an amazing patience; to my twin brother, Robert, who endured my journey with both loving guidance and encouragement; to my son, Benicio, who reminds me daily why what we do matters; and to my parents, Leland and Tina Bassett, for the inspiration gained from their tireless work to improve the human condition and for the lessons learned from them as they continue to fight for the human spirit and potential.

I wish to also acknowledge Peter Ndenga, whose rare intelligence and talents inspired me as a teenager and who was taken from us far too soon.

The guiding mentor through all of this has been Dr. Curtis L. Ivery, who dedicates his life every day to cultivating the liberating freedom that comes from education and to inspiring each of us to dare to dream, to seek that dream, and to pass it on to the next generation.

Joshua A. Bassett
Detroit, 2011

FOREWORD

Once again, Dr. Curtis Ivery has proven himself to be a fierce and ardent critic of American social ills. With courageous candor and a journalist's eye, he has helped to create a compelling argument for change and has issued a profound call to action. *America's Urban Crisis and the Advent of Color-Blind Politics: Education, Incarceration, Segregation, and the Future of U.S. Multiracial Democracy* represents his "prodigious gift" for assessing the multiple barriers facing cities, which have historically remained entrenched sites of poverty, incarceration, unemployment, illiteracy, and racial segregation. In its unique critical framing of these issues to both general and specialized audiences, the book makes a valued contribution to the field of urban underclass theory.

Dr. Ivery explores systemic problems in areas that were once pockets of vitality, enterprise, and innovation but now have descended into "urban hells." In a series of provocative discussions, this collection illustrates the paradox of apathy, failed race relations, and governmental corruption and negligence sustaining America's urban crisis. It addresses the economic and moral breakdown that has threatened sustainable living and resulted in deflated opportunities and decades of suffering. Those sentiments, which are expressed throughout the book, represent what one critic calls a "running commentary on the national arc of sorrow."

Yet, Dr. Ivery offers hope. With penetrating insight and scholarly acumen, he transcends the pathology of despair and presents persuasive arguments for achievement and meaningful social change. In the process, he shares a wide-ranging and humane civic vision and raises the national debate on urban chaos to a new level.

His central project is to reclaim the project of integration and the language of race itself from the hegemonic influence of U.S. "color-blind" theory and politics, which he argues have not only debilitated the efforts of urban communities to empower themselves across a broad spectrum of economic and educational indices but have also masked how such indices continue to be influenced by race, that is, continue to reflect how social conditions are *racialized*.

Ivery contends that solutions can only be reached by revisiting "the policies and attitudes of the past that remain part of the problem today." An outspoken proponent of "creative approaches" to entrenched dilemmas, he stresses the need for groundbreaking remedies. "If we keep doing the same thing, we'll keep getting the same results," he states.

Dr. Ivery assembled an esteemed group of scholars, journalists, public officials, and artists to assess this conundrum and respond to the historical and contemporary challenges that stand in the way of the empowerment of ordinary citizens. The sum of this effort—and its contribution to the field of urban studies—can be derived in this book's unifying thesis that offers a comprehensive understanding of America's pitfalls.

The second chapter, "Color-Blind Ideology and the Urban Crisis," is the central organizing essay of this volume and asserts that "color-blind ideology," which was most formally advanced politically during the Reagan administration and manifested into law under the Bush/Cheney regime, has become the dominant paradigm through which all aspects of America's urban crisis must be considered. Chapter 3, "Mass Incarceration and the Urban Crisis," considers the vastly destructive consequences that the U.S. prison-industrial complex has disproportionately caused to urban communities, particularly in terms of education and core efforts of revitalization. Chapters 4 and 5 focus on what leading scholars have identified as the re-segregation of America's public school system and its debilitating effects on urban areas—more than fifty years after the promise of *Brown v. Board of Education*, which outlawed legal segregation but has proven to be one of the great failures of American democracy. Chapter 6 extends the question of racial equality in the context of America as a newly emergent "multiracial democracy" and further examines this important concept in relation to voting and civic disenfranchisement. The concluding chapter, "Toward Solutions to the Urban Crisis," considers initiatives in educational institutions and related community programs that can promote healthy urban dynamics and economic opportunities.

This book is a provocative examination of a multidimensional crisis and a gold mine for all who know and understand that the future of America, and the world, rests upon the future of urban centers.

We ignore this fateful truth at our own peril.

Cornel West

PREFACE

My own personal experience with racism and segregation began while growing up in Texas in the 1950s and 1960s, where racial discrimination was seen as a logical consequence of human nature, a so-called choice that people made to "be with their own kind," rather than a legal construct that imposed social divisions and inequality. Yet, for me, racism also offered a window into the soul of a society living in the contradiction of its own history—a history founded upon slavery and predominant views of racial superiority that for centuries made hollow its written constitution that declared equality and justice for all.

Watching America as we know it today, much of our racial history seems an afterthought, with a clear majority of our population subscribing to the specious idea that the nation has become, for all practical intents and purposes, "color-blind." Consequently, the inequalities that exist are deemed the result of individual failures and not the collective practices of our history.

In many areas throughout the United States, it is understandable why the belief that we've entered a truly "color-blind era" has taken hold. Certainly, as the historic election of Barack Obama as the first African-American president of the United States demonstrates, race relations in the nation have significantly improved in the last half-century, and the economic conditions for African Americans,

Latinos, Asians, and other non-white communities have also, albeit unevenly, progressed. These facts, taken with the unprecedented visibility of minorities in our mass media and popular culture, have, as many scholars have noted,[1] contributed to the perception that America has resolved its discriminatory past and achieved a state of genuine equality. Yet, in vast areas across the United States, particularly in the nation's inner cities, the idea that we've entered a truly color-blind era that affords equal opportunity for all is a fantasy that ignores the reality of what has for decades been defined as the "crisis in urban America"—generational conditions of concentrated poverty, unemployment, segregation, incarceration, inadequate education, and related ills, which have disproportionately afflicted African American, Latino, and non-white populations.

In no place is this crisis any more apparent or historically significant as it is in my home city of Detroit. In a span of ten years, from 1970 to 1980, Detroit underwent an unprecedented racial transformation from being a majority white city, with an overall population of approximately 1.5 million residents, to being a majority black city, with an overall population of approximately 1.2 million residents—a figure that also represents an exodus of 1.1 million whites from the city since 1950.[2]

When I moved to Detroit in 1995, I had a great appreciation of the city's history just after the First World War as a gateway of hope and opportunity for tens of thousands of blacks seeking to escape Jim Crow politics of the South for the promise of good-paying automotive factory jobs and broader social freedoms. Despite the familiar practices of racial discrimination that still dogged black populations who had relocated to Detroit, blacks still made remarkable progress on many fronts, including the establishment of vibrant cultural and economic enclaves within the city and their integral involvement in the major civil rights movements of the 1960s.

But today, much of the progress that African Americans, Latinos, and other historically marginalized communities made after the advent of the 1960s civil rights movements has slowed and even regressed in many respects. In Detroit, for example, African Americans and Latinos still rank below their white counterparts on nearly every level of socioeconomic status, and the region as a whole is the most segregated racially and economically of any area in the nation. Detroit is not unique in this respect. Most major cities in America today remain largely segregated along lines of race and class, particularly in the nation's public school systems, which despite the genuine advances made by certain segments of African-American and Latino communities, have returned to levels of segregation not seen since the 1960s.[3]

Beyond these voluntary forms of segregation—for it is a choice that our civic and social institutions have so far done little to change these dynamics—the subject of race relations remains a crucial issue for our nation, especially during the course of the next several decades, when the United States will for the first time in its history, no longer be composed of a majority white population. Looking back on a related historical transformation, namely my experience of public education in Texas in the aftermath of *Brown v. Board of Education*, it's important to observe that while that landmark case did in fact change access to public education, it did not significantly affect the social norms of the day. In almost all respects, black communities continued to have to endure inequalities in education, employment, and access to goods and services, and while our classrooms eventually began to integrate, we still lived the same separate social lives that we did prior to *Brown*.

Today, some fifty years after *Brown*, this social separation continues to be a defining feature of American life, which if left unchecked, will continue to divide our many diverse communities and undermine the basic principles of democracy that represent the ideals of our nation. It is for this reason then that America's urban crisis has become a key issue of our times that calls for no less than a national dialogue on race relations and commitment to integration not seen since the great civil rights movements of the 1950s and 1960s, when Americans came together across lines of race, religion, class, and gender to collectively unite in support of racial and civic equality.

Our efforts here represent just one small step in this otherwise profound national project, which will again require our collective will as a society to be successful. The many noted contributors participating in this book have provided a framework in which educators, business and civic leaders, and all persons concerned about the welfare of their communities can engage critical urban issues in accessible and effective ways. To this end, the chapters of this book focus on familiar aspects of America's urban crisis, including its origins and the role of segregation in its perpetuation, as well as more recent scholarship that considers the effects of the U.S. criminal justice system and practice of mass incarceration on urban dynamics, the advent of the so-called color-blind era in U.S. racial politics and its relevance to the urban crisis, and the related concepts of multicultural public education and multiracial democracy in America.

I want to extend my sincerest thanks and admiration to all the contributors, who made this book possible, and to their own respective and important commitment to improving our collective social condition and the very nature of our democracy itself. I'd also like to extend a special thanks to my co-editor and critical race scholar, Josh Bassett, for his invaluable efforts in developing the thesis of this project, and to consulting editor Stephen J. Kasser, who offered valued insights. Josh and I also wish to honor the recent passing of Manning Marable and express our greatest admiration for his brilliant work and deserved legacy as a truly influential figure in the history of civil rights in America.

Though our work often seems to produce the most fragile kinds of progress, our efforts must always be unyielding.

Curtis L. Ivery
Detroit, 2011

NOTES

1. See, for example, *White Out: The Continuing Significance of Racism*, edited by Ashley "Woody" Doane and Eduardo Bonilla-Silva (New York: Routledge, 2003).

2. The *Detroit News* and U.S. Census Bureau statistics. In 1970, Detroit's white population was approximately 800,000, while its black population was approximately 650,000. In 1980, the figures were approximately 750,000 blacks and 400,000 whites.

3. Erica Frankenberg, Chungmei Lee, and Gary Orfield, "A Multiracial Society with Segregated Schools: Are We Losing the Dream?" (Los Angeles, Calif.: The Civil Rights Project at the University of California at Los Angeles [UCLA], January 16, 2003). www.civilrightsproject.ucla.edu.

1

INTRODUCTION
and Theoretical Overview

This book developed as an outcome from a series of ongoing educational initiatives based in Detroit, including two national conferences held in the city during the last several years: "An Educational Summit: Responding to the Crisis in Urban America" (2002) (which was broadcast on C-SPAN) and "Rebuilding Lives: Restoration, Reformation, and Rehabilitation in the U.S. Criminal Justice System" (2004). Both address what scholars from a broad range of academic fields have long defined as the "crisis in urban America."

The book is an attempt to frame the insights gained from these efforts, using analyses by leading scholars, media, and educational figures, in a context that can be useful to the wide range of entities dedicated to improving the lives of urban communities, which continue to be disproportionately affected by enduring cycles of unemployment, concentrated poverty, illiteracy, incarceration, segregation, and related crisis conditions.

It is further an attempt to extend the discussion of the state of America's inner cities into new dimensions, informed by recent historical and political events and advances in scholarship, and to outline a multidisciplinary framework in which potential solutions to the causes and consequences of the crisis in urban areas may be developed and implemented on both a local and national scale.

Broadly, our work here will contribute to existing scholarship and analysis of America's urban crisis in the following ways:

1. Focusing on the role of "color-blind ideology" and its related frameworks, as a means to examine and redress the maintenance and perpetuation of American urban crisis conditions.
2. Examining the practices and policies of America's criminal justice system and its role in fomenting the urban crisis.
3. Considering the role of multicultural education in responding to the current operations of the U.S. public school system, which some fifty years after *Brown v. Board of Education*, remains highly segregated and continues to perpetuate urban inequalities.
4. Expanding on familiar debates on the causes of America's urban crisis beyond structural versus personal/cultural models to include influential work in the academic fields of race and ethnic studies, specifically as related to theories of "racial formation" and color-blind ideology.
5. Extending the focus from the traditional white-black binary of U.S. racial politics to an expanded discussion of multiracial identity politics, including Latino, Asian, Arab, and other non-white communities and their positions within the urban crisis.
6. Theorizing the future role of race in U.S. democracy in the context of projected Census demographics, which predict that by 2042, white populations in the United States will no longer be a majority for the first time in the nation's history.

We will begin with a brief review of three key works on urban issues that frame our overall analysis. Much seminal analysis has been done on what has happened to America's inner cities, and much of it has centered on Detroit, which because of its distinct racial and economic histories, stands at the epicenter of America's urban crisis.

In *The Origins of the Urban Crisis: Race and Inequality in Postwar Detroit*,[1] Thomas Sugrue chronicles Detroit's descent from its 1940s status as America's "Arsenal of Democracy" and the fifth-largest city in the United States, with a population of nearly two million, to its present-day status as a city with a population of under one million that continues to be plagued by "joblessness, concentrated poverty, physical decay, and racial isolation" (p. 3).

> Over ten thousand houses are uninhabited; over sixty thousand lots lie empty, marring almost every city neighborhood. Whole sections of the city are eerily apocalyptic. Over a third of the city's residents live beneath the poverty line, many concentrated in neighborhoods where a majority of their neighbors are also poor. A visit to the city's welfare offices, hospitals, and jails provides abundant evidence of the terrible costs of the city's persistent unemployment and poverty. (p. 3)

While the extreme degree of Detroit's problems is in many ways unique (and will be considered further in our analysis), Sugrue argues that the city's current conditions and their historical causes are reflected throughout the United States, particularly in the formerly vibrant manufacturing centers in cities such as New York, Baltimore, Pittsburgh, Philadelphia, Cleveland, Chicago, Saint Louis, and related areas that now collectively form America's Rust Belt:

> The urban crisis is jarringly visible in the shattered storefronts and fire-scarred apartments of Chicago's South and West Sides; the rubble-strewn lots of New York's Brownsville, Bedford-Stuyvesant, and South Bronx; the surreal vistas of abandoned factories along the waterfronts and railways of Cleveland, Gary, Philadelphia, Pittsburgh, and Saint Louis; the boarded-up and graffiti-covered houses of Camden, Baltimore, and Newark. (p. 3)

How and why these formerly vital economic centers transformed into geographies of prolific urban decay in the relatively short time span from the 1950s to the present day is the fundamental question of Sugrue's work, and his analysis of Detroit within this context stands as the primary case study for any comprehensive understanding of the current state of America's urban crisis and the development of effective interventions to respond to its continued damaging effects on the nation.

CAUSES AND CONSEQUENCES

Sugrue identifies three dominant theories of the "urban underclass" that attempt to explain the causes and effects of America's urban crisis. The first and "most influential" theory, according to Sugrue (and, we would add, most problematic),[2] focuses on cultural values and behaviors of low-income communities and the effects of federal social programs on "fostering a culture of joblessness and dependency in inner cities" (p. 4). The second theory focuses on structural explanations that consider the historical impact of economic practices and continuing forms of racial discrimination and segregation on low-income urban communities. The third critical view identifies dominant politics and social policies that were *reactionary* responses to the 1960s civil rights movements, urban rebellions, and the inception of affirmative action programs as the cause of the deterioration of formerly vibrant urban areas into areas beset by cyclical conditions of segregation, unemployment, incarceration, and inadequate public education.

Sugrue's own analysis favors structural explanations for America's urban crisis, and he advances these theories by more critically focusing on issues of race, housing, and labor and their interrelations and effects in producing underclass urban populations. He argues that contrary to most accounts, America's urban crisis did not in fact begin in the 1960s with the advent of the civil rights movements and racial activism, both violent and nonviolent, but rather originates decades earlier in the 1940s and 1950s as a result of "a multiplicity of structural forces" that limited the abilities of primarily low-income African-American communities to improve their lives through economic, educational, and political resources, a dynamic that can also be related to current conditions afflicting many Latino communities in the United States.[3]

In terms of housing, Sugrue points to federal housing policies such as the GI Bill that provided affordable mortgages to white populations just after World War II, while denying such mortgages to blacks on the basis of discrimination, as well as dominant real estate, lending, and legislative practices that worked to ensure massive widespread residential racial segregation throughout the United

States. Sugrue also extends this analysis of residential segregation to the concept of the physical space of cities and suburbs themselves and the question of how spatial relations inform social perceptions and broader race relations today. Sugrue's examination of the development of Detroit's freeway systems in the late 1940s is an important example here because their construction not only exacerbated residential segregation between Detroit's black and white populations but also fueled social and political divisions as well.

> Beginning in the late 1940s, the most densely populated sections of black Detroit were devastated by highway construction. The Oakland-Hastings (later Chrysler) Freeway blasted through the black Lower East Side, Paradise Valley, and the Hastings Street business district, wiping out many of the city's most prominent African American institutions, from jazz clubs to the Saint Antoine branch of the YMCA. The John C. Lodge Freeway cut through the Lower West Side, the increasingly black area bordering Twelfth Street, and the heavily black neighborhoods bordering Highland Park. The Edsel Ford Freeway, an extension of "Bomber Road," which connected Detroit to the Willow Run defense complex west of the city, bisected the black West Side, and cut through the northernmost fringe of Paradise Valley. (p. 47)

This destruction of vital black economic, residential, and cultural centers in Detroit via the freeway systems had significant consequences on racial and class inequalities in the city and its emerging metropolitan suburban enclaves. In terms of race, the expanding spatial divisions between city and suburbs enhanced already prevailing stereotypes of racial identity, which historically viewed black populations as inherently less intelligent than whites and naturally self-destructive. This, in turn, influenced attitudes toward segregation itself, which instead of being seen as an antidemocratic practice, could now be explained as a logical consequence of racial difference.[4] Economically, the great irony of the development of Detroit's freeway system, which was conceived during the heights of the city's prosperity, is that it paved the way for Detroit's substantial population exodus (and subsequent economic decline), while at the same time providing the tax base and capital that would make the very wealth of the majority white suburbs possible.

Sugrue's exhaustive study of Detroit provides key insight into familiar social narratives that still stand as fundamental dividing points between Detroit and its metropolitan suburbs. These narratives, which are articulated through media, social, and civic discourse, relate to enduring debates on the causes of America's urban crisis, particularly in terms of whether urban underclass conditions are driven by culture/behavior or are the logical consequence of historical structures of inequality.

In the context of present-day Detroit/metro-Detroit relations, the colliding views of this debate were actually crystallized in the historical time period of the early 1970s, when Coleman A. Young was elected Detroit's first black mayor and blamed by former majority white populations for destroying the city because of his alleged racism toward whites. Conversely, for Detroit's new majority black populations, the election of Young, who had a brilliant record of civil rights achievements before becoming mayor, represented the most significant exercise of their democratic power within a long and violent history of racial discrimination.

Sugrue's work raises important questions, which are considered by numerous contributors to this book, especially as they relate to issues concerning the structural causes of America's urban crisis. In the case of Detroit (and in cities throughout the United States), a key question we wish to examine is, given this obvious history of structural discrimination exacted against black populations in the city, what are the forces at work that have minimized this history in the minds of primarily white suburban populations, who continue to blame Detroit's ills on the failure of black populations to effectively govern? Moreover, what constructive means can be undertaken to find a common ground between these divergent views of the city (and nation) in order to achieve a healthy and mutually beneficial interracial future?

FARLEY, DANZIGER, AND HOLZER

A second influential work that sets a context for our efforts is Reynolds Farley, Sheldon Danziger, and Harry J. Holzer's *Detroit Divided*.

Their study of Detroit is part of a broader examination of America's urban crisis that also includes the cities of Boston, Atlanta, and Los Angeles. A key point in their work, as in Sugrue's, is the question of the causes of urban underclass conditions, which the authors similarly pose in the theoretical context of economic inequalities and racial discrimination versus cultural values and behavior. As with Sugrue, Farley, Danziger, and Holzer favor structural explanations for perpetuating race and class inequalities and focus on the "long-term interplay of four processes: historical trends, changing labor markets, persistent residential segregation, and pervasive racial animosity and mistrust" (pp. 5–6). The authors write that while these processes similarly afflicted cities throughout the United States, their effects on Detroit were most severe because of the unique economic and racial histories of the city. They state that Detroit's emergence in the early twentieth century as the automobile capital of the world had the adverse consequence of restricting the economic diversity of the city, preventing it, unlike other major U.S. cities, from becoming "a dominant center for trade, financial services, higher education, entertainment, or government" (p. 6). Further, the authors point to highly discriminatory immigration laws during this period, as well as virulently racist Jim Crow policies in the South (which were also operant in the North), as fostering conditions wherein unprecedented numbers of black populations migrated to Detroit—more than any other northern city in the United States—for the promise of economic and civic empowerment. This unrivaled influx of black populations in Detroit was, predictably, not received well by white majorities in the city and produced dynamics of racial conflict and division that Farley, Danziger, and Holzer claim are unequaled in U.S. history and have led to making present-day Detroit and metro Detroit the most racially and economically segregated region in the nation.

Farley, Danziger, and Holzer's analysis of Detroit affirms much of Sugrue's historical studies of segregated housing and land-use practices, as well as offering a more extensive examination of unequal labor dynamics in understanding the causes of the city's racial divisions and economic decline. For our purposes, it is their research and sociological surveys of contemporary racial attitudes of black and white communities in terms of residential living that raise key questions about the future of race relations in Detroit and metro Detroit—questions that must be expanded to include the ever-increasing Latino, Arab, and Asian populations in the region.

In their surveys of racial attitudes of black and white residents in Detroit and metro Detroit, Farley, Danziger, and Holzer note that while "much progress" has been made in race relations since the late 1920s, when the Ku Klux Klan was a potent force in Detroit's politics, and the 1960s, with the eruption of violent racial conflicts, there still remain strongly polarizing racial views between black and white communities that continue to sustain the historical dynamics of residential segregation:

> Whites increasingly endorse the principle of equal racial opportunities . . . [and] recognize the continued existence of frequent racial discrimination in the metropolis, but place much less emphasis on it as the primary cause of the problems of blacks. Instead many whites endorse the idea that Detroit blacks are neither working very hard nor taking advantage of opportunities open to them. . . . [Moreover] when we asked whites questions about the modern racial stereotypes—that is, about racial differences in the tendency to be intelligent or the tendency to prefer to live off welfare rather than to work for a living—we found that a majority [of whites] still endorse negative stereotypes. (pp. 10–11)

These stereotypes obviously affirm cultural/behavioral explanations for urban crisis conditions and no doubt play a key role in understanding why, despite improved race relations, many whites still will not move into integrated neighborhoods.[5] The authors also extend their studies to the question of blacks' views of residential integration and stereotypes of white communities to more effectively identify the causes of persistent residential segregation. In researching the living preferences of blacks, Farley, Danziger, and Holzer take issue with recent accounts by scholars such as Stephan and Abigail Thernstrom and Orlando Patterson, who argue segregation persists in large part because "blacks are unwilling or reluctant to move into white neighborhoods" (p. 201). Rather, the authors report that blacks "clearly prefer [to live in] racially mixed neighborhoods" (p. 201) and, significantly, that blacks reject stereotypes that are based on ideas that link race and intelligence (p. 227).[6]

Farley, Danziger, and Holzer's research into the racial attitudes of black and white communities toward integration is important to consider in developing a program of solutions to abate racial divisions in Detroit/metro Detroit; however, their work does not address how these racial attitudes interplay within a multiracial context of the region's increasing Latino, Arab, and Asian populations. While research in this area both locally and nationally is limited, recent studies suggest there is an emerging racial hierarchy at work in majority white neighborhoods, wherein white populations are more tolerant and accepting of certain races than others. For example, in their analysis of the highly influential Multi-City Study of Urban Inequality (MCSUI), Maria Krysan and Camille Zubrinsky Charles indicate that whites are most comfortable living with Asian populations, less comfortable with Latinos, and least comfortable with blacks.[7] The reasons that motivate this hierarchy of racial tolerance are no doubt complex and, we argue (as do others),[8] can be related to racial stereotypes and their effects on social attitudes. Given that the populations of non-whites will only continue to increase across the nation—indeed the states of California, Texas, New Mexico, and Hawaii are now majority Latino, African American, Asian, and others—examining this phenomenon in much more extensive detail is crucial to cultivating a more tolerant and democratic society.

PROGRESSIVE STRATEGIES

Farley, Danziger, and Holzer outline four major strategies by which Detroit/metro Detroit can begin to effectively resolve its significant race and class inequalities and move toward a more progressive and beneficial future. These strategies focus on developing economic and educational practices that among other influences, will effect positive population trends in the arenas of housing and employment and will in turn lead to more integrated and favorable race relations and dynamics. The four strategies are defined as follows:

1. "Labor Market Supply-Side Strategies." These efforts would focus on developing close relationships between employers and educational institutions to improve economic opportunities for low-income populations, as well as developing more cooperative relationships among high schools, community colleges, and universities to this effect.
2. "Mobility Strategies to Link Firms and Workers." These strategies would focus on (a) integrative housing policies, (b) economic incentives for businesses not only to locate in degrading urban areas but also to play a role in encouraging local entrepreneurship within communities, and (c) public transportation policies to facilitate employment access.
3. "Labor Market Demand-Side Strategies." These strategies would involve already successful enterprise zones in urban areas, which encourage the establishment of businesses and steady employment opportunities. They would also include "Employment[s] of Last Resort," which would provide temporary jobs to low-income persons unable to find adequate employment.
4. "Antidiscrimination Strategies." Such strategies would involve educational, civic, community, and business entities working collaboratively to emphasize the substantial and collective economic and social benefits of racial integration as a key goal for the region.

We will consider these strategies in more detail via the analyses of our contributors and the last section of our book, "Toward a Solution to the Urban Crisis."

OMI AND WINANT

A third key text that informs our efforts is *Racial Formation in the United States: From the 1960s to the 1990s*, by Michael Omi and

Howard Winant (New York: Routledge, 1994). While Omi and Winant's work in this volume does not provide a direct case study, as do Sugrue and Farley, Danziger, and Holzer, of a major city through which the crisis in urban America can be examined, their analysis of the historical development, operations, and effects of U.S. racial politics on producing America's urban crisis is among the most influential within academic studies and is crucial to understanding the political processes by which predominantly black, Latino, and non-white communities continue to be most afflicted by debilitating urban conditions.

For the purposes of our analysis, we will focus on two key areas of Omi and Winant's work. The first concerns the very concept of race and racial identity in the United States, which the authors argue must be reframed if we are to meaningfully address the racial divide that still defines the geography, if not the social fabric, of the nation. The second identifies the dominant paradigm or ideology in which our present-day "commonsense" understanding of race and race relations operates, namely, as noted, the color-blind era of racial politics, whose ascendance Omi and Winant locate in the 1970s and 1980s, primarily with the election of former Hollywood actor Ronald Reagan as U.S. president and the rise of neoconservatism as a dominant political discourse.

To begin to reframe our general understanding of race, of how we think and talk about racial identity and race relations in our communities and in the context of our national politics, Omi and Winant examine three major epochs in the "evolution of modern racial awareness" (p. 61) that have most influenced dominant Western social views.

Broadly stated, the first epoch, which originated approximately in the sixteenth century during the European colonization of the Western Hemisphere, defined race primarily in religious terms as a "natural" concept that distinguished Europeans from all other human beings, as the highest forms of human life. Such beliefs engendered numerous hierarchical perceptions of identity, including a caste system defined by skin color (e.g., the lighter one's skin, the more intelligent and superior; the darker, less intelligent and inferior), and were often used to rationalize the genocide and/or expropriation of indigenous peoples.

The second epoch, which occurred during the eighteenth and nineteenth centuries, advanced on this religious/natural concept to define race as a scientific and biological category, wherein leading scientific theories were used to explain and justify innate or "essentialist" differences between the races, which accounted for their alleged disparities in intelligence, behavior, and capabilities.[9] This scientific epoch of racial understanding, although now widely discredited, still influences contemporary ideas of race and remains a significant obstacle to improving urban conditions and race relations in the United States.

The third and most recent epoch of modern racial thinking emerged during the twentieth century and directly opposes the previous eras by regarding race as a social and political construction without any biological basis.[10] This epoch marks a significant advancement in the history of our understanding of race and is now the overwhelmingly dominant view within academic institutions and professional scholarship, yet it remains a problematic concept to many communities which, however supportive of democratic ideals, still, on some level, regard racial differences as explanations for a broad range of urban inequalities.

Recognition of race as a social/political construct rather than an innate biological condition should in theory provide a framework to effectively address issues of racial inequality, racism, and race relations as a whole. However, the influence of this development on U.S. racial politics—according to Omi and Winant, particularly in the early 1960s via the work of Nathan Glazer and Daniel Patrick Moynihan (*Beyond the Melting Pot*, 1963) and later in the 1980s and early 1990s during the ascendance of neoconservative and "New Right" (p. 134) political views of race (e.g., Ronald Reagan, Clarence Pendleton, William Rusher, etc.)—has instead promoted a now dominant color-blind perspective of racial identity that, while offering some measure of racial progress, has in general foreclosed productive dialogues on race and done little to abate persistent conditions of the urban crisis that disproportionately afflict non-white communities (pp. 145–146):

> Optimistic observers . . . often acknowledge past [racial] atrocities, but offer a vision of the contemporary U.S. as an egalitarian society, one which is trying to live up to its original principles by slowly extending and applying them to the gnawing issue of race. . . . The "color-blind" society, it is argued, will be the end result of this process. Yet viewed more deeply, recent history—particularly the period from the 1960s to the 1980s—reveals a more complex and contradictory trajectory in which the pattern of race relations seems far less certain, and much less tranquil. (pp. 1–2)

Omi and Winant identify an influential period of the political institutionalization of the color-blind era with the election of Ronald Reagan as U.S. president in 1980. During his administration, he made the incredible claim that the United States had achieved racial equality (p. 5) and pursued a civil rights platform promoted by his then chair of the U.S. Commission on Civil Rights, Clarence Pendleton, that was based on eliminating race-conscious policies such as affirmative action in order to create a "color blind society that has opportunities for all and guarantees success for none" (p. 1).

While the ideals of a color-blind society may seem admirable, Omi and Winant argue that under the Reagan Administration such efforts were actually highly race conscious and driven by a reactionary view that civic policies developed in the 1960s to remedy centuries of racial discrimination had in the 1980s transformed into policies that directly discriminated against white populations: "Under the guise of creating a truly 'color-blind' society, [Reagan] administration officials sought to define and eliminate the 'new racism' against whites. As Reagan's U.S. Civil Rights Commission Chairman Clarence Pendleton, Jr. characterized it, the new racists were 'supporters of civil rights' who 'exhibit the classical behavior system of racism. They treat blacks differently than whites because of their race'" (p. 135).

The argument that progressive race-conscious policies are tantamount to "reverse discrimination" represents one of several significant ways by which "neoconservatives" and the "New Right" shaped U.S. racial politics during the 1980s and even influenced Democratic views on such matters in the early years of the Clinton administration in the 1990s (pp. 135, 147). Other key effects that Omi and Winant ascribe to neoconservative/New Right policies on racial politics during this period, which we will argue exerted substantial influence via the Bush/Cheney administration, include:

1. Reframing dominant U.S. social views of race and specifically racial inequalities from matters of collective interest—as was the case in the 1960s, when Americans across lines of race, class, gender, and religion collectively opposed racial politics that were deemed antithetical to a democracy—to matters of individual interest, which mitigate the historical effects of institutional discrimination and promote the false idea that the United States, for all intents and purposes, has achieved racial equality.

2. Establishing the era of "reverse discrimination," especially as it affects white males, and promoting the widespread social view that all races are equally affected by forces of discrimination—which both ignores the distinct forms of oppression experienced by respective racial groups (e.g., the genocide of Native Americans, mass enslavement of Africans, colonization of Mexicans, exclusion of Asians, etc.) and perpetuates racial and/or cultural explanations for inequalities that disproportionately afflict racial communities.

3. Influencing "Neo-Liberal" (p. 147) racial politics during the Clinton/Gore administration, which, while certainly differing from earlier color-blind neoconservative policies, nonetheless avoided "framing [such] issues or identities racially" (p. 148). This approach, which neo-liberals argue is necessary to remedy urban inequalities in a social/political sphere that is hostile to direct addresses of race, remains within current progressive civil rights communities a key point of contention, with significant factions arguing that the language of race must not be abandoned in strategic efforts to achieve racial equality.[11]

4. Providing a key foundation that we argue allowed the Bush/Cheney administration's program to expand color-blind policies in its legal opposition to all forms of affirmative action

(including efforts to redress glaring educational inequalities), its opposition to voluntary public school desegregation programs (despite massive segregation in U.S. public schools), and its failure to engage the nation in any meaningful discussion of racial politics that would build common ground between communities that hold highly polarized views of race.

The central thesis of Omi and Winant's work is that color-blind theory and politics cannot effectively address contemporary U.S. racial dynamics and that new approaches are required if we are to resolve critical issues of race that continue to divide the nation and sustain a wide spectrum of inequalities that define America's urban crisis (p. 145). In rejecting color-blind ideology, Omi and Winant make an important contribution to decades of critical studies of race by developing what they define as the theory of "racial formation" and its related concept of "racial projects"(pp. 55–56).

RACIAL FORMATION AND RACIAL PROJECTS

Omi and Winant call for no less than a new social understanding of race that will allow the United States to effectively engage racial issues that continue to fuel inequalities, as well as move beyond what they describe as the "prevailing bipolar/[binary] black/white model of race relations" (p. 153), which is obviously inadequate to addressing racial politics as they affect the ever-increasing and diverse racial communities in the nation (e.g., Latinos are now the largest non-white population in the United States) and, we will argue, counterproductive to developing what scholars define as a "multiracial democracy," a concept we discuss in more detail in Chapter 6 of this text, "Multiracial Democracy and the Urban Crisis."

To lay the foundation for a new social understanding of race, Omi and Winant advance on previous scholarship that has defined race as a social and political construct by further considering the concept as a "matter of both social structure and cultural representation" (p. 56) that can "facilitate understanding of . . . the relationship of race to other forms of differences, inequalities, and oppression such as sexism and nationalism, and the dilemmas of racial identity today" (p. 56). Omi and Winant describe this approach as the theory of racial formation, which they assert "emphasizes the social nature of race, the absence of any essential race characteristics, the historical flexibility of racial meanings and categories . . . and the irreducible political aspect of racial dynamics" (p. 4). The authors specifically define racial formation as "the sociohistorical process by which racial categories are created, inhabited, transformed, and destroyed" (p. 55) via "historically situated [racial] projects" (p. 55). A "racial project," according to Omi and Winant, is "an interpretation, representation, or explanation of racial dynamics, and an effort to reorganize and redistribute resources along particular racial lines" (p. 56). These projects, which we are all subject to on a regular basis, play a crucial role in defining what race "means in . . . both [our] social structures and everyday experiences" (p. 56).

The theories of racial formation and racial projects are important to our analysis in several ways, which will be detailed further, but our main emphasis is that racial formation offers an important critical tool to address biological and/or stereotypical views of race that still permeate common understandings of racial dynamics and thereby fuel urban crisis conditions. The concept of racial projects further allows us to identify and examine the way racial dynamics inform and structure our social and political relations in an era that may yet be influenced by the recent historic election of Barack Obama as president of the United States but otherwise attempts to render such dynamics invisible.

THESIS AND CHAPTER OUTLINES

We have organized the articles and commentaries of our contributors around five key areas of analysis that, we argue, are central to a more comprehensive understanding of America's urban crisis; its often cyclical and disproportionate effects on black, Latino, and primarily non-white and economically disadvantaged communities;

and the development of potential strategies and solutions that can be useful in responding to degenerative urban conditions that persist in urban areas throughout the nation.

While our efforts here do not provide an exhaustive theoretical and/or research analysis of the five specific areas of examination considered in the respective chapters of this book, we do believe that our contributors offer useful outlines to address these matters in ways that will advance scholarship in the field of urban studies across numerous disciplines and that will develop into more academically specialized research methodologies and theoretical paradigms. Because our contributors reflect a broad spectrum of social positions, including mainstream media figures (both print and television), political leaders, civil rights activists, and professional scholars, their commentaries range from academic, journalistic, and political to personal accounts of America's urban crisis, which are intended to be accessible and useful to both general and specialized audiences who share a common engagement with urban issues.

The five key areas of analysis around which this book is organized are described as follows:

Chapter 2, "Color-Blind Ideology and the Urban Crisis," broadly outlines various facets of color-blind ideology and its effects on America's urban crisis. This chapter considers both the structural operations and social effects of color-blind views of U.S. race relations and argues that efforts to effectively respond to urban inequalities on a national level must involve a direct address of prevailing color-blind policies that continue to sustain key foundations of America's urban crisis.

Chapter 3, "Mass Incarceration and the Urban Crisis," considers the current operations of the U.S. criminal justice system and its wide range of effects on perpetuating the urban crisis. This chapter considers the often overlooked collateral consequences of mass incarceration in the United States, which now has the largest prison population in the world,[12] on non-incarcerated populations and also focuses on how a "prison-industrial complex" has developed within the United States as a result of the dominant criminal justice practices.

Chapter 4, "Segregation and the Urban Crisis," broadly outlines the persistent effects of social and institutional segregation on the urban crisis but expands familiar discussions beyond traditional divisions between black and white communities to consider how segregation influences social relations among numerous racial communities whose populations continue to increase in the United States. This chapter also considers how political policies after 9/11 have influenced prevailing views of Arab-American communities and their broader social relations.

Chapter 5, "Education and the Urban Crisis," examines the continuing segregation in America's public school system and its role in sustaining critical structures of urban inequalities, including, importantly, a "school-to-prison pipeline," which has emerged in the last several decades in the United States. This chapter will also consider various means by which educational institutions and interest groups may reclaim integration as a central tenet of public education, more than fifty years after *Brown v. Board of Education.*

Chapter 6, "Multiracial Democracy and the Urban Crisis," examines the concept of "multiracial democracy" and its emerging relevance in relation to America's urban crisis. This chapter considers the mechanisms by which non-white communities continue to be most severely affected by the dynamics of the urban crisis and consequently limited in their ability to participate in the democratic process.

Our concluding chapter, "Toward Solutions to the Urban Crisis," identifies key points of analyses of our contributors that can be developed into potential approaches aimed at resolving key facets of America's urban crisis. This chapter also discusses programs and initiatives conducted in Detroit that may also serve as models for productive urban engagement throughout the nation.

NOTES

1. Thomas J. Sugrue, *The Origins of the Urban Crisis: Race and Inequality in Postwar Detroit* (Princeton, N.J.: Princeton University Press, 1986).

2. Michael Omi and Howard Winant offer an incisive critique of "pathological" explanations of urban inequality in *Racial Formation in the United States: From the 1960s to the 1990s* (New York: Routledge, 1994), pp. 14–25. Eduardo Bonilla-Silva extends this analysis in his conception of "cultural racism" as a foundational paradigm of "color-blind racism," in *Racism Without Racists: Color-Blind Racism and the Persistence of Racial Inequality in the United States* (New York: Rowman & Littlefield, 2006), pp. 25–52. Our key concern here is that contemporary cultural explanations for urban inequality can be seen as nonracist because they apparently have no affiliation to antecedent biological explanations of racial inequality (e.g., the racist, but formerly widespread, belief that blacks are biologically less intelligent than whites). We would argue, however, that cultural explanations of urban inequality *always* presume a biological component.

3. Bonilla-Silva offers a fine overview of these dynamics in his chapter, "The Strange Enigma of Race in Contemporary America," in *Racism Without Racists*, pp. 1–24. Also, see Edward Murguia and Tyrone Forman, "Shades of Whiteness: The Mexican American Experience in Relation to Anglos and Blacks," in *White Out: The Continuing Significance of Racism*, edited by Ashley "Woody" Doane and Eduardo Bonilla-Silva (New York: Routledge, 2003), pp. 63–81.

4. Bonilla-Silva defines this view of segregation as the color-blind frame of "naturalization," wherein segregation is seen as "natural because people from all backgrounds 'gravitate toward likeness'" (*Racism Without Racists*, p. 28).

5. Maria Krysan provides valuable research here in "Whites Who Say They'd Flee: Who Are They, and Why Would They Leave?," *Demography* 39(4) (November 2002), pp. 675–696.

6. Farley, Danziger, and Holzer report that while "many whites reject the stereotype that there are racial differences in intelligence [between themselves and blacks] . . . [t]he majority—52 percent of whites—ranked their own race higher than blacks"(*Detroit Divided*, New York: Russell Sage Foundation, 2000, p. 223). A key point to be examined here is how the social construction of racial identity functions in terms of racial stereotypes and the consequent effects of such stereotypes on a particular racial group. We would argue, for example, as Richard Dyer suggests in his influential work on white identity, *White: Essays on Race and Culture* (New York: Routledge, 1997), that social constructions of whiteness tend to be uninfluenced by stereotypes that would otherwise negatively impact non-whites.

7. See Krysan, *Demography*, pp. 675–696; and Camille Zubrinsky Charles, "Can We Live Together?: Racial Preferences in Neighborhood

Outcomes," in *The Geography of Opportunity: Race and Housing Choice in Metropolitan America*, edited by Xavier de Souza Briggs (Washington, D.C.: Brookings Institution Press, 2005), pp. 45–80.

8. See Krysan, *Demography*, pp. 675–696; Zubrinsky Charles, *The Geography of Opportunity*, pp. 45–80; Murguia and Forman, *White Out*, pp. 63–81; and Farley, Danziger, and Holzer, *Detroit Divided*.

9. The term "essentialist" here more appropriately applies to contemporary theoretical analyses of identity and identity politics. See, for example, Diana Fuss, *Essentially Speaking: Feminism, Nature, and Difference* (New York: Routledge, 1989).

10. For a more detailed analysis here, see Omi and Winant, *Racial Formation in the United States*, pp. 53–91.

11. john powell, director of the Kirwan Institute for the Study of Race and Ethnicity, has written and lectured substantially on this matter. See www.kirwaninstitute.org.

12. Marc Mauer provides a detailed examination of these statistics in *Race to Incarcerate* (New York: The New Press, 2006).

2

COLOR-BLIND IDEOLOGY
and the Urban Crisis

For the purposes of our thesis, we argue that the five key areas of analysis of America's urban crisis discussed by our contributors are also informed in dominant social and political terms by color-blind ideology. We frame our overall analysis with an examination of the color-blind era because, as leading scholars note,[1] color-blind theory and politics inform most social perceptions and discourses on race and race relations in the United States today and thus operate as critical structures that influence all aspects of America's urban crisis.

Drawing from Omi and Winant's theory of racial formation and racial projects, we argue that color-blind ideology operates in both representational and structural terms[2] and during the last three decades, has produced, as noted, a now dominant social belief that racial inequalities and racial discrimination no longer exert any relevant influence within social and civic life in the contemporary United States. Sociologist Eduardo Bonilla-Silva has written extensively on this phenomenon, which he defines as "color-blind racism" (or the practice of "racism without racists"),[3] and drawing upon both qualitative and survey research, including a 1998 study of Detroit populations (i.e., Detroit Area Study [DAS],[4] developed what he identifies as the four central "frames"[5] that sustain U.S. color-blind ideology. Bonilla-Silva defines these frames as follows: "abstract liberalism," "naturalization," "cultural racism," and "minimization of racism" (*Racism Without Racists*, p. 26).

While a detailed discussion of these frames is beyond the scope of this chapter, their key ideas as they relate to urban issues and broader race relations are familiar in general social discourse and take the following forms:

"Abstract liberalism" refers to fundamental notions of equality and, for example, prevailing views that affirmative action and related progressive race-conscious policies are themselves forms of discrimination that are antithetical to democracy. Bonilla-Silva notes that such views require ignoring and/or minimizing the historical effects of legal discrimination on non-white communities, as well as, most importantly, how current practices of civic and social segregation continue to sustain racial inequalities (*Racism Without Racists*, p. 28).

The frame of "naturalization" concerns seemingly commonsense ideas that all races "naturally stick to their own kind" and thus segregation itself is a natural phenomenon without institutional and/or ideological basis. This frame accords with, as noted previously, now discredited biological views of race, which, however, continue to inform general social perceptions of race relations.

"Cultural racism" reflects a departure from biological views of race, which, historically, for example, held that blacks (and other non-whites) were less intelligent than whites, to embrace the idea that it is the culture of minorities itself that is responsible for sustained urban inequalities. This frame, in our view, still incorporates a biological component to race (e.g., what is responsible for this "difference in culture"?) but enables, as Bonilla-Silva asserts, the position that racial inequalities are a consequence of culture, not race (*Racism Without Racists*, p. 29).

Lastly, "minimization of racism" concerns key ideas that racism and discrimination are conditions that occurred centuries ago and/or in the faraway past but in contemporary America, no longer exert any meaningful consequence on non-white populations, a view that, as noted, requires cultural/biological explanations to account for educational, economic, and civic inequalities that are oriented by race.

The following articles/commentaries by our contributors in this chapter provide further insight to Bonilla-Silva's four central frames of color-blind ideology, as well as those representational and systemic structures that sustain such ideology. This insight, of course, is crucial if we are in fact to develop a new language and dialogue of race to effectively address America's urban crisis.

COLOR-BLINDNESS, RACISM, AND MULTIRACIAL DEMOCRACY

by Michael Omi

Michael Omi's essay offers an insightful and accessible analysis of how language functions to sustain the dominance of color-blind social beliefs and civic policies, particularly in terms of general understandings of the concepts of race and racism. A key argument he makes is that while color-blind ideology has functioned to render race as an irrelevant social/political category, there has also been an effective effort to limit the conception of racism itself almost exclusively in terms of "hate" and "irrational" behavior. Such views are extremely problematic to arriving at a common ground from which to engage issues of race relations and racial inequalities in several important ways.

First, denying that racial identity still has relevance in the United States is to negate the reality of many non-white communities, who, as noted, are disproportionately affected by inadequate educational, economic, and institutional resources and who commonly experience discrimination as a salient feature of their social lives.[6] Moreover, in terms of civic agency, notwithstanding the genuine progress that the Obama presidency represents, unacceptable levels of underrepresentation of non-whites in local, state, and federal governments still remain, including, in our view, most significantly in the U.S. Senate and Republican body of the House of Representatives. Incredibly, the Senate includes no African-American members (which is fewer than during the Reconstruction Era) and only two Latinos, while the GOP House membership includes but two African-American congressional representatives.[7]

Reducing the concept of racism to hate and/or aberrant psychology also forecloses potentially constructive interracial dialogues because, as Omi observes, racism is removed from any context of "power," or more specifically, civic/institutional structure, the effect of which subsumes the role of race in relation to one's access to opportunity (e.g., education, housing, financial resources, etc.), as

well as oversimplifies how racism operates in a multiracial society.
Related to this point, Omi also importantly addresses the concept
of multiracial democracy, which will be further discussed in Chap-
ter 6, and its relevance in U.S. race relations/politics.

A reporter once told Malcolm X that the passage of civil rights legislation was clear proof that things were getting better for blacks. In
response, Malcolm X said that it did not show improvement to stick
a knife nine inches into someone, pull it out six inches, and call it
progress. You had to pull the knife out and heal the wound it left.
"But some people," Malcolm X observed, "don't even want to admit
the knife is there." That's our problem today. Many whites, and
some people of color, believe that the goals of the civil rights movement have been achieved, that racial discrimination is a thing of the
past and that we are now a truly color-blind society. The "knife" of
racism—persistent forms of structural inequality that are based on
social concepts of race—is ignored. Race-conscious remedies, policies, and practices (e.g., affirmative action, minority set-asides, and
redistricting strategies) are increasingly critiqued, contested, and
dismantled for being, in an interesting and ironic twist, "racist."

The reigning racial ideology in our country today is that of "color-
blindness." A pervasive belief exists that the most effective antiracist
gesture is simply to ignore race, as the often-repeated mantra goes,
"I don't care if someone is black, white, yellow, green, or purple. I
treat all people the same." Increasingly, individuals deny that skin
color informs our perceptions, shapes our attitudes, and influences
our practices. The result is to deny that race matters.

In advancing its claim that race does not matter, color-blind ideology strategically evokes the fact that there is no biological reality to
the concept of race. While biological and genetic arguments regarding racial "difference" continue to surface, such notions have been
roundly discredited in the sciences. But having been challenged as
a "scientific" category, race is now regarded as a questionable social
category—a myth that perpetuates forms of false (racial) consciousness. For over a year, the American Anthropological Association, in
response to the President's Initiative on Race, engaged in a vigorous

debate regarding whether the concept of race retains any meaning at all as an analytic social category, when biological definitions have been so thoroughly discredited. Race becomes a suspect category—a ghostly apparition—that clouds rather than illuminates social relations and the patterns of social stratification.

Coupled with the disavowal of race as a legitimate social category is the incessant call to "get beyond race"—to "get over it." The use of the "race card" in politics has been roundly criticized from positions across the political spectrum. Some on the political Right, such as Dinesh D'Souza, have proclaimed the "end of racism," while condoning forms of "rational discrimination." Progressives bemoaning the weakness of the American Left, such as Todd Gitlin, have accused identity-based social movements of "essentializing race" and subverting the advancement of a universal political subject and unified political movement. From this perspective, race is a smoke screen—something that detracts our collective attention away from "real" issues such as class-based economic inequality and the perils of globalization.

But contradictions abound. While the concept of race is increasingly disavowed in popular political discourse, we continue to witness the use of coded language and symbols that evoke and play upon racial meanings without explicit reference to race. Such ploys have a long history. Dearborn mayor Orville Hubbard's campaigning in the 1940s to "keep Dearborn clean," for example, was certainly a thinly veiled plea to "keep Dearborn white." Issues of crime, welfare, drug use, real estate values, and the quality of public schools, among others, are highly racialized but are often talked about without recourse to naming or referencing race. East Detroit's name change to Eastpointe, in 1992, speaks to the manipulation of coded language—in this instance, to the process of imagining and defining residential space in racial terms.

Contributing to the ascendance of color-blind ideology in the current period is a significant political movement to ban the collecting of racial demographic information. Examples are numerous. Certain states and local governments do not cooperate with the voluntary provisions of the Hate Crimes Statistics Act. Prior to his fall from grace, Newt Gingrich supported a multiracial category on the Census as a way to illustrate the indeterminacy of all racial categories and thereby argue for their abolition. In California, Ward Connerly placed a Racial Privacy Initiative on the ballot. This measure would have amended the California Constitution to prohibit "the act of separating, sorting or organizing by race . . . including, but not limited to, inquiring, profiling, or collecting such data on government forms."[8] The problem here is that without some form of racial classification and record keeping, we are unable to empirically observe institutional patterns of racial inequality, with respect to income, education, and health care, among other important indicators of well-being and life chances. Though the Fair Housing Act of 1968 made it illegal for lenders to use race as a basis for lending decisions, it was not until the 1980s that data-collection laws were passed and lending patterns could subsequently be discerned. It was found that loan-rejection rates were twice as high for blacks as for whites with similar income profiles. Racial categories, however flawed and imprecise, and racial data are crucial to discern the scope and magnitude of social inequality. While color-blind ideologues seek "racial privacy" from the state, the reality remains that we don't have such privacy when applying for a job, renting an apartment, or driving down the highway.

One of the ironies of the post–civil rights era is that while formal legal equality has been significantly achieved in many institutional arenas, substantive racial inequality remains and, in many cases, has deepened. Persistent forms of racial inequality are, however, rendered invisible by the ideology and language of color-blindness. Like the concept of race, the term *racism* is increasingly considered to be bereft of meaning and analytic utility. What does the term *racism* mean when a wide range of attitudes and practices—from individual acts of prejudice to institutional forms of discrimination—all potentially fall under its rubric? The problem of conceptual inflation and its political consequences is a real concern. I am worried that the term *racism* in popular political discourse is increasingly subject to conceptual deflation, meaning that what is considered racist is being narrowly defined in ways that obscure rather than reveal the pervasiveness of racial power in our social order.

CHAPTER 2

Critical race scholar David Theo Goldberg makes the point that in the last decade or so, racism has been popularly conceived of as hate. The category of "hate crimes" has been introduced in many states as a specific offense, with enhanced sentencing consequence, and many colleges and universities have instituted "hate speech" codes to regulate expression and behavior both inside and outside of the classroom. Dramatic acts of racial violence are given considerable play in the mass media and are the subject of extensive condemnation by political elites.

The reduction of racism to hate, however, both conceptually and politically limits our understanding of racism and the ways we can challenge it. Racist acts are seen as "crimes of passion"–abnormal, unusual, and irrational deeds that deeply offend our collective morality. Missing from such a narrow interpretation of racism are the ideologies and practices in a variety of institutional arenas that reproduce racial inequality and domination. For example, less attention, if any, is given to the racist dimensions of public school funding or access to health care.

We need to expand our understanding of racism as power. Part of the challenge is to create a more precise language and appropriate concepts to examine specific aspects of racial power and how they are experienced by, and affect the overall life chances of, individuals and social groups. Racism is expressed differently at distinct levels and sites of social activity over historical time, and we need to be attentive to its shifting meaning in various contexts. Rather than imagining a single monolithic racism, we need to envision multiple forms of racism and how they structure different aspects of our lives and relations with others.

Such a concept of racism will be crucial to envisioning and moving toward a multiracial/multicultural democracy. A starting point for dialogue between different racial groups is to acknowledge the historical and contemporary differences in power that different groups possess. Groups are positioned in unequal ways in a racially stratified society. In a study of perceived group competition in Los Angeles, sociologists Lawrence Bobo and Vincent Hutchings found, among other things, that whites felt least threatened by blacks and most threatened by Asians, while Asians felt a greater threat from blacks than from Latinos. Such distinct perceptions of "group position" are related to and implicated in the organization of power.

In the transition to a multiracial democracy, some widely accepted verities will need to be critically examined. Many scholars and activists, for example, have defined racism as "prejudice plus power." Using this formula, they argue that people of color can't be racist since they don't have power—but things aren't that simple. In the post–civil rights era, some groups of color have carved out a relative degree of power in specific urban areas and have been instrumental in, among other things, the administration of social services and distribution of economic resources. In cities such as Oakland and Miami, this has led to conflicts between blacks and Latinos over educational programs, minority business opportunities, and political power, with dramatically different results depending on which group held relative power. This is not to dismiss the overarching reality and hegemony of white supremacy, but it does suggest that confronting and acknowledging the differences in racial power that groups possess will be a crucial first step in addressing racism.

Unfortunately, we remain a nation in denial. We are in denial about the extent of our racial problems and the roots and historical trajectory of those problems. It's increasingly difficult to talk about race in the classroom, in the workplace, and in the electoral arena. People don't want to hear about racial privileges and disadvantages, about how we are collectively implicated in the prevailing racial order: "I'm not responsible for slavery," "Every person has a chance to make it on their own merits," and "We shouldn't give any special preferences based on race." All these arguments are familiar. The forms of racial inequality we see in Detroit and other major cities in our nation are not understood in relation to racial advantages that some groups have historically accrued. These advantages include, among others, the availability of home loans, decent job opportunities, health care access, and favorable suburban transportation policies. These advantages have created long-term and persistent forms of racial inequality. In assessing the contemporary "playing field," we need to recognize race, not ignore it.

Let me end with a nod to the Motor City. According to ethnic studies scholar George Lipsitz, Malcolm X used to say this to his followers: "Racism is like a Cadillac, they bring out a new model every year." The racism of 1952 is not the racism of 2002. I'm arguing that in current dialogues and debates, we need to be attentive to the lines and features of the new model. A pressing need exists to challenge the current appropriation of civil rights discourse under the guise of "color-blindness" and at the same time, frame a new language, a new way to talk about race, that explicitly confronts the nature of racial power in our society and advances new principles of social justice.

"DIFFERENCE," EMISERATION, AND AMERICA'S URBAN CRISIS

by Houston Baker

In this essay Houston Baker forcefully outlines historical founda-
tions of racial inequality in the United States and directly relates
them to current ideological and institutional forces that sustain
core conditions of America's urban crisis. His analysis importantly
links the relationship between racial ideology and real-world
practices and posits that the systemic marginalization of minor-
ity communities within the United States originates within the
context of identity politics, wherein non-white populations are
defined fundamentally in "difference" from their white counter-
parts. In the color-blind era of U.S. racial politics, however, this
process is inverted, and historical "differences" of racial identity
are supplanted by the prevailing social view that people are "all
the same" despite sustaining racial inequalities that operate on
almost all social and economic levels. Baker further exposes how
these racial inequalities operate outside the United States and in a
transnational context, the consequence of which has produced an
unprecedented global underclass.

Today's urban crisis is the logical, historical, political, economic, and educational extension of the national operation of race in America. In the context of the United States, race reads as follows: after one apprehends *difference*, one establishes a grid of differentiation. It reads "superior/inferior," "civilized/savage," and most importantly, in the United States, "white/black." Once the grid is in place, dynamics of racism begin to unfold in economic exploitation; legal subordination; physical brutalization; and the spatial, political, and educational separation of those designated "other."

To think of the United States—whose colonial history includes the extirpation of Indians and chattel enslavement of Africans—without granting premier place to racism is like thinking of Harvard without Puritanism or Catholicism without sacramentalism. I believe the two aspects of American racism that are most useful as we seek to address the so-called urban crisis are incarceration and emiseration. From the holds of slave ships and the eternally surveilled and brutalizing slave-coast barracoons of various European powers, to Southern plantations and into the impoverished enclaves and ghettos of southern and northern areas—where urban blacks have always been scandalously overcrowded—black bodies have been subjugated and locked down. Today, the intricate network of the U.S. prison-industrial complex inescapably arrests us. American racism has immemorially swept black bodies into incarceration.

Point two: *Emiseration.* It endures, as the black majority continues to receive the poorest goods and services in America. At the same moment, the black majority is subjected (eternally) to horrific white physical violence, represented in its worst early-twentieth-century manifestations by spectacle lynching and in its present-day lows and ignominies by the fates of Rodney King, James Byrd, Jr., Amadou Diallo, and countless thousands of nameless others who are racially profiled, randomly street-stopped, humiliated for the offense of MWB: *moving while black.* Blacks, since the beginning of American history, have been the all-too-human twin towers of the United States, murdered by missiles of white terror.

We must pay attention to movement. Whites have always pathologically feared black mobility. For whites, it is equivalent to "terrorism," unless the black movement is that of exile or deportation. To come upon a bleak midwestern Rust Belt landscape such as Detroit—a landscape characterized by zones of black confinement and immobility, marked by a total inadequacy of goods and services, and populated by a black majority that is vastly unemployed and routinely subjected to violence—is not to encounter a *new American crisis.* It is to behold what a defining white American racism has made of our national identity. That pure, horrific product of racism is metro Detroit and enclaves like it across the United States. Detroit's blight and violence, inequality and misery do not so much exhibit America caught in unfamiliar crisis, as they reveal America splayed and displayed in its national operational *norms.* At least this is true with respect to the black majority, which has never lived well in the United States.

The black novelist Richard Wright was an exemplary chronicler of urban crisis. His 1940 novel *Native Son* was both a report and portrayal of crisis, and a forecast of the devastating effects of slums for the national polity. Set in Chicago, *Native Son* focuses on the slums of the South Side and the psychology that emanates from the offices of *Real Estate*. The protagonist, Bigger Thomas, and his family of four pay eight dollars a week to live in one rat-infested, unventilated room in a blighted building located in a crime-ridden, densely populated, and pathetically underresourced neighborhood. The Thomas family's existence is controlled by Dalton Real Estate, which bears the name of its chief shareholder, a rich white man who lives in a mansion on Drexel Boulevard. It is the Daltons who, through the offices of social welfare, give Bigger a job as chauffeur—part of their philanthropy toward the Black World—but things go very badly.

After driving the Dalton's daughter, Mary, and her boyfriend around Chicago for an evening, Bigger returns the young girl to her home. She is too inebriated to walk. He carries her to her bedroom but is surprised by the sudden appearance of her mother in the doorway. Bigger puts a pillow over Mary's face to keep her silent, fearing Mrs. Dalton will find his presence *criminal*. Mary suffocates, and Bigger is suddenly a murderer on the run. At his trial, his Communist defense lawyer, Boris Max, interrogates Mr. Dalton about the cause and effect of Mr. Dalton's "ownership" and exploitation of the Thomas family. Max knows that Mary's death is a violent return upon the violence of capitalist *Real Estate* and its "holdings." In his essay, "How Bigger Was Born," Richard Wright observes: "I sensed, too, that the southern scheme of oppression was but an appendage of a far vaster and in many respects more ruthless and impersonal commodity-profit machine." The global linkage is here. In the American South, for Wright, there were the "Lords of the Land." In the North, there are the "Bosses of the Buildings." Both sets are monarchs of *Real Estate*. Their dynamics of power and ownership are transgeographic. They find their "modern" origins in the Transatlantic Slave Trade and its entailments. The Transatlantic was the *Ur*-commodity-profit machine of Capitalism. In its latter-day urban Detroit and Chicago manifestations, desolation, displacement, violence, and despair are ghostly and traumatic returns upon those ships' holds and plantation economies, which in the words of Toni Morrison, "broke the world." The slums are avatars of Transatlantic ownership, racialization, and violent displacement. Wright's Black Urban Chicago is a forecast of the state of our world today. In his book *Planet of Slums* (New York: Verso, 2006), Mike Davis writes the following:

> Altogether, the global informal working class (overlapping with but non-identical to the slum population) is about one billion strong, making it the fastest-growing, and most unprecedented, social class on earth. . . . Among researchers, there is a base consensus that the 1980s crisis—during which informal-sector employment grew two to five times faster than formal-sector jobs—has inverted their relative structural positions, establishing informal survivalism as the new primary mode of livelihood in a majority of Third World cities. (p. 178)

Agrarian subsistence enterprise (such as "sharecropping") is disrupted by highly mechanized corporate agribusiness. The impoverished seek refuge in cities. Erstwhile communally organized rural domains become depopulated targets of predatory armies (e.g., Ku Klux Klan and Janjaweed Militia). The armies are in service to the state, or merely nonuniformed civilian thugs, purveyors always of what scholar Achille Mbembe, in his compelling study, *On the Postcolony* (Berkeley: University of California Press, 2001), calls "necropower" (p. 173).

Displacement to urban domains yields the intense marginality of smokestacks, ashes, and the vicious unpredictability of the informal economy, meaning illegal vending, sweatshops, unregulated day labor, unlicensed transport, sex trade, and narco-trafficking. Displaced millions migrate daily in search of minimal recompense and a square of earth to sleep. Davis writes: "Instead of cities of light soaring toward heaven, much of the twenty-first-century urban world squats in squalor, surrounded by pollution, excrement, and decay.

. . . By 2015 Black Africa will have 332 million slum-dwellers, a number that will continue to double every fifteen years" (*Planet of Slums*, p. 19).

"Bigger," the name Wright chose for his protagonist in *Native Son*, was not accidental allegory. Race and displacement are monumental and omnipresent. Slums and their inhabitants are *bigger* and far more disastrous in our century than Wright could have imagined. Idealism, desire, and expressive brilliance were his stock-in-trade, seasoned with a Marxist intonation. He believed if he wrote passionately and analytically enough, people would listen, and change. However, he knew indisputably that transatlantic *Real Estate* had produced a "Negro" and a "Negro Condition," which are metaphors for global race and displacement. War, incarceration, and chaos were standard processes of the Transatlantic. They continue in the slum economies of our millennium.

In the absence of economic reparations, urban reform, and global governmental and juridical reconciliation, what end can our century anticipate? *Planet of Slums* concludes with a meditation on military and think-tank scenarios on the future of urban slums. Mike Davis provides a vision of apocalyptic urban conflict. To the end of time, slum "insurgents" battle military counterinsurgents of the formal economy. *Native Son* concludes in less sensational fashion. Sentenced to death by the court, Bigger sits on a cot in Chicago's Cook County Jail. His idealistic defense lawyer has departed: "[Bigger] held on to the bars. Then he smiled a faint, wry, bitter smile. He heard the ring of steel as a far door clanged shut." This is Wright's prophetic ending. Today, the trajectory of Black Urban Crisis for slum dwellers is *school, drop out, incarceration, death*. The cycle is not accidental or inexplicable; it is a direct descendant of the Transatlantic and its incumbencies. The U.S. Black Urban Majority inhabits slums. It is, therefore, a bitter irony of our times that the election of America's first black president has been heralded as the beginning of a "postracial era."

SURE, WE'RE ALL JUST
ONE BIG HAPPY FAMILY[9]

by Benjamin DeMott

DeMott provides important insight into the actual mechanisms by which representations function to produce color-blind discourse, and his work can be related to critical studies in the fields of film and representational semiotics, as well as more survey-based sociological analyses of race.[10] His thesis derives from his original conception of narratives of "racial sameness," which he asserts emerged as a common feature in American film and television in the 1990s and have been influential in promoting false ideas that the United States has achieved racial equality. DeMott further argues that these narratives of racial sameness have limited the nation's ability to engage in meaningful discussions of race because they propose that all races share a common and unified view of American social and political life, uninfluenced by historical forces of discrimination and/or contemporary racial inequalities.

Though DeMott's essay originally appeared in 1996, it was developed more extensively in his later work.[11] We include it in our collection because of its relevance to current practices of racial/ multiracial representation in popular media, as well as political discourse, particularly in terms of the 2008 presidential election, wherein Barack Obama's successful candidacy was hailed by many as the dream of a color-blind nation fulfilled.[12]

For a moment—the moment of the verdict in the Simpson trial— white America discovered race difference. Film and photographs of the reactions to the words "not guilty" proved that blacks and whites don't see things the same. Troubled citizens spoke in shock— on televised "town meetings" and call-in radio shows, and in letters to the editor about the gap between the races. "As blacks exulted at Simpson's acquittal," wrote Henry Louis Gates Jr. in The *New Yorker,* "horrified whites had a fleeting sense that . . . blacks really were strangers in their midst." Why are blacks and whites so divided?

COLOR-BLIND IDEOLOGY AND THE URBAN CRISIS

Repeatedly posed, this question was nevertheless vacuous. What needed serious inquiry were other questions: Why are whites so dim about the division between the races? What forces, what processes, lulled white America into assuming that blacks and whites were ever on the same page?

One answer is clear. Over the last generation, this country's politics and pop culture have relentlessly sold the notion that the races have achieved equality and are the same. For an assortment of reasons, a great many Americans have bought the scam. Our most powerful media images depict black-white sameness. They are feel-good images. They fail to connect with the texture of city life familiar to the 60 percent of black Americans who have not reached middle-class status: the life of the projects, or of the jobless, the homeless and the illiterate. And they do not begin to reflect the deep conflicts of opinion between American blacks and whites at every class level.

The media images I speak of, remote from urban fact, have been teaching mass audiences everywhere that race differences belong to the past, that inequalities of power and status and means have disappeared, that at work and play blacks are as likely as whites to be found at the top as at the bottom and that the agency responsible for the creation of near-universal black-white sameness—the only agency capable of producing progress—is that of friendship between the races.

Naturally the images teach without sermonizing. No preacher interrupts the NBC feed on weekdays at 6:59 A.M. to intone with podium sonority that a minute hence *The Today Show* will conduct a morally improving demonstration of interracial collaboration and equality in action to which all right-feeling, God-fearing viewers should devotedly attend. Bryant Gumbel and Katie Couric, firm friends, simply show up, cozily communicating mutual enjoyment (Katie on occasion answers Bryant's teasing with a gentle nudge to his side). There is no competitive wariness or boss-underling antsiness; recurring casual remarks suggest familiarity with each other's after-hours pleasures and irritations.

In place of a lecture about black-white equality and sameness, *Today* brings to life a version of the thing itself, presenting it every weekday morning as the national norm. And thereafter come blizzards of sameness and sympathy narratives—talk shows, sitcoms, cop shows, commercials, late night. Prime time, all the time. In the hit NBC series *Seinfeld*, George struggles to show his black boss that he's capable of winning and keeping a black friend. On *Designing Women*, now in syndication on Lifetime, Anthony and Julia, black and white business partners, reveal how sympathy and affection cause race differences to vanish in the Atlanta environs. On *Murphy Brown*, Candice Bergen comes to like and admire a new network executive, a black man who initially seemed threatening; the two make common cause for "standards."

On cartoon shows, jokes and gimmicks regularly highlight black-white palship. When Freddie Flintstone of *Flintstone Kids* takes a picture with his Polarock camera, a bespectacled black buddy is featured prominently.

Switch channels—to reruns or what you will. On *Doogie Howser, MD*, the teenage doctor hero is held hostage in a drugstore holdup but—here's street life loud and bold—he not only makes friends with the black teenager who's threatening him but also suggests the possibility of a hospital job. Persuaded by his new buddy, the hoodlum releases the hostages and turns himself in. On *L.A. Law* a young black lawyer whose mother opposes his love affair with a white woman explains, "Mom, the reason I love her is that inside she's just like you."

Jessica, a black lawyer on the CBS soap *As the World Turns*, marries white, debonair Duncan. On the talk show *Later*, Camille Paglia compares herself to Anita Hill. At all hours of the day and night a black woman and a white woman (Dionne Warwick and Linda Georgian) converse companionably on the Preview channel, talking up the Psychic Friends Network. Black and white buddy stars—Billy Crystal, Robin Williams and Whoopi Goldberg—are co-hosts for HBO's annual *Comic Relief* telethon. HBO's *Dream On* chronicles the black-white friendship of Martin Tupper (Brian Benben) and Eddie Charles (Dorien Wilson).

Commercial content matches program content. Tonight's good-buddy blacks and whites discuss, in pairs, the virtues of products ranging from Cadillacs to Tylenol. (The black half of each pair usually explains the superiority of the product.) Yesteryear's memorable pitchmen-sidekicks included Kareem Abdul-Jabbar and Larry Bird, who chummily chaffed each other while explaining the virtues of Lay's potato chips. The old cronies exited together, a makeup cap on Larry's head redoing them into interchangeable, dome-headed twins.

Round the clock, ceaselessly, the elements of this orthodoxy of sameness are grouped and regrouped, helping to root an unspoken but felt understanding throughout white America: race problems belong to the passing moment, race problems do not involve group interests and conflicts developed over centuries, race problems are being smoothed into nothingness, gradually, inexorably, by good will, affection, points of light.

Race-deleting themes in the movies are uncommonly various. At times—see *Pulp Fiction*—interracial sameness emerges in contexts of violence and amorality. At times the good news is delivered through happy faces, loving gestures, memorable one-liners. Tom Hanks as Forrest Gump loses his beloved best buddy, a black soldier (Mykelti Williamson), in combat and thereafter devotes years to honoring a pledge made to the departed. In *Driving Miss Daisy*, rich Jessica Tandy turns to Morgan Freeman, her poor black chauffeur, and declares touchingly, "You're my best friend, Rob."

At times, scene and action hammer home the message of inter-racial sameness; mass audiences see individuals of different colors behaving identically, sometimes looking alike, almost invariably dis-covering, through one-on-one encounter, that they need or delight in, or love, each other.

Danny Glover sits on the toilet in *Lethal Weapon*, trousers around ankles, unaware of a bomb ticking below him; Danny's white buddy, Mel Gibson, breezily at home in Danny's house, saves his life by sweeping him from the throne to the tub. Minor and major films show well-off white grownups unhesitatingly helping young blacks. In *Dangerous Minds*, Michelle Pfeiffer selflessly teaches black youngsters, using Bob Dylan songs to hook them on poetry. *Philadelphia* plumbs the friendship of two lawyers—white, AIDS-afflicted Tom Hanks and black, spiky Denzel Washington. (Joanne Woodward as Hanks's mother underlines the black-white sameness theme: "I didn't raise my children," she says angrily, "to ride in the back of the bus.")

A monograph on the history of race-sameness themes in movies would reach back to breakthrough works like *The Defiant Ones, Brian's Song, Guess Who's Coming to Dinner*, and *Hurry Sundown*. A hint of the quantity of relevant "product" can be gleaned from an almost random list of recent films—television and junk action movies mingling with more pretentious work—that treat friendship themes for part or the whole of their length. They range from *The Shawshank Redemption* to *Fried Green Tomatoes*, from *Sister Act* to *Platoon*, from *Die Hard with a Vengeance* to *Angels in the Outfield*, from *Clockers* to *Clueless* to *Smoke* to *Money Train*.

Nor is it the case that black-white sameness is a staple only of the more mindless entertainment and sales pitches. Admittedly the most vulgar dramatizations of the theme turn up on dirty-talk shows: Rolonda, Ricki, and their peers encouraging utterly undifferentiated whites and blacks to wallow in aberrationist muck. And it's true, too, that the grubby opportunism of the theme is least well-disguised in the Wal-Mart fliers that jam rural and suburban mailboxes, pairing, on every page, black and white models who glow in each other's company.

But friendship and sameness themes actually respect no class or "intellectual" border, appearing often in the work of PBS essayists and longtime liberal heroes. Studs Terkel opens his book *Race* by recommending a program of "affirmative civility," meaning, efforts by whites to reach out with genial evening greetings when passing blacks on city sidewalks. Discussing his son's warm friendships with blacks, Roger Rosenblatt declares, "Our proper hearts tell the truth, which is that we are all in the same boat, rich and poor, black and white."

Why has white America bought so enthusiastically into race-friendship, race-sameness orthodoxy? The problem is complex; spelling out possibly adequate answers has taken this writer an entire book, *The Trouble with Friendship*.

The country is wedded to an egalitarian, individualistic, can-do, making-it mythology, the American Dream, that's meant to leave nobody out. The country is keen on historical romance, impatient with historical fact, weak on the realities that uniquely characterize the African-American past. Pop versions of history (*Roots*, Ken Burns's *Civil War*, movies like *Mississippi Burning*) are therefore at liberty either to delete the experience of separateness altogether or to transform slavery and the civil rights movement into periods of happy black-white collaboration.

Neoconservatives are troublingly eager to exaggerate the size and rate of expansion of "the new black middle class," and liberals are astonishingly tolerant of politically calculated exploitation of friendship dogmas. President Clinton is among those who have found that trumpeting black-white amity as a "solution" is a convenient and economical way of dramatizing one's "concern"; it wins praise for sensitivity. No need to confront the hard truth that a caste society attempting erratically to dismantle its caste structures can't expect to get the job done without making commitments to developmental assistance on an order this country has never imagined.

Beyond these explanations of white receptiveness to sameness-and-sympathy dogma stands the complicating truth that friendship ideas do, after all, represent a step forward from yesterday's race-viciousness. Combined with an intelligent address to the problems of non-middle-class blacks, the friendship faith could move us toward a positive interracial future. Some sameness themes radiate real moral energy and carry an inspiring, even lyric charge. You can hear the promise ring out in black-white duets— Aretha Franklin and George Michael, or Conway Twitty and Sam Moore sharing choruses of "A Rainy Night in Georgia"—or in the Garth Brooks song about learning to ignore "the color of skin" and looking for "the beauty within!"

But if there's some decency as well as vast nonsense in the ideology of sameness from which, for a week or two last Fall, white America seemed almost to awaken, there's also fearful obliviousness. What whites need to do is stop being amazed at their own obliviousness and start being repelled by it and by the opinion engineers whose difference-abolishing pap still plays cover-up with cruel, hope-erasing race matters as they are.

IMMIGRATION, EDUCATION, AND THE MEDIA

by Maria Hinojosa

*Maria Hinojosa, former CNN reporter and current host of Na-
tional Public Radio's* Latino USA, *offers a personal commentary
on her work as a Latina journalist living in the United States
attempting to report the stories of the "voiceless in America." She
also discusses her own educational experience and how current inequalities in the U.S. public school system (which will be addressed
in detail in Chapter 5) continue to impede the overall progress of
black and Latino urban communities within the nation. Her observations here raise familiar, though often uncritically analyzed,
questions about why certain non-white communities (e.g., Indian,
Asian, West African), at least statistically,[13] are more successful
economically than others (e.g., African American, Latino, American Indian)—a social outcome that in many discussions of the
urban underclass belies how historical operations of discrimination do not affect races equally[14] and contribute to stereotypes of
minority communities (e.g., the "model" Asian as compared to the
"lazy" black, etc.), the latter of which Hinojosa also addresses.*

*A key point that Hinojosa makes concerns the structural opera-
tions of race within mainstream media (in contrast to DeMott's
analysis of visual representations) and the role urban communities and their allies (from all geographies) can play in influencing
media narratives of urban conditions.*

There are those in our country who seek division and have created
an idea that black Americans have stolen the American dream. I
would say the attacks now are not limited to blacks. Immigrants,
including Latinos, are also blamed for stealing the American dream.
They are accused of stealing jobs, privileges of citizenship, and good
education away from their children, who are now sometimes forced

---

This essay is based on a speech delivered by Ms. Hinojosa in 2002.

to deal with multilingual or bilingual programs in their schools. The anger has created a backlash movement to ban bilingual education in states, as in Arizona. The anger is so real now that if people could vote immigrants out of the United States, they probably would.

Anger at the growing demographic changes in this country is not subtle. It is a full frontal attack against educating these people—the "communities" that are accused of stealing away all that was once good, pristine, controllable, and "monolithic" about these United States.

On a personal note, I want to share my own story. I did poorly on my SAT scores. For years, it was a silent and painful secret I kept. I am not saying anyone should strive to get low SAT scores or be proud, as our current president [former president Bush] said, to be a C+ student. What I am saying is that poor SAT scores had nothing to do with my graduating magna cum laude from Barnard College. My educational success had everything to do with working and studying incredibly hard and understanding that I would have to work three times as hard as my Anglo counterparts.

And I still do. Now, though, I work hard to tell the stories of the voiceless in America. Following is an example of one of these stories.

I thought about what happened after September 11: the children of the victims who lost their lives have been told they will get access to a free college education, which is really wonderful. The problem is that the victims whom I have met range from every possible background you can imagine. It is unrealistic to believe that just by promising these children they're going to go to college for free they are somehow guaranteed to make it through the next eight or ten years in school to make it to the point where they are ready for college. The challenges in grade school or high school can be huge.

With that in mind, I'm going to tell you the story of Julia Hernandez, whose husband, Antonio Melendez, worked at the Windows on the World restaurant. He was at the restaurant and died that day, leaving four children and Julia, living in the Bronx. His best friend, whom he brought with him to find a job that day, left four children and a wife in Mexico. Julia's oldest child is undocumented, as is

Julia, as was her husband. Her children are not given any special treatment in their school because they lost their father.

I went to visit the family one day and picked the children up from school: Marco, seven; Yaritza, eight; and Daisy, twelve. When we got to their home and were settled in, I asked them how it was going for them in school. After a pause, Daisy told me that Marco had had to defend her because she was going to get into a fight.

Pero como? "How is that possible?" I asked. They told me they're all being teased because their father died on September 11. Unfortunately, that is the reality of so many of our children: when they are at school, they have no one to defend them. They do not have SWAT teams to protect them and propel them forward.

In the media, unfortunately, the crisis we all know exists is invisible, because the media is run by a small homogeneous group of very wealthy men for whom this is not a crisis. They don't experience an educational crisis for their kids, and therefore, some may even question how severe the crisis is. Why run a series on education on your news network if it won't get good ratings?

That situation is not going to change for a long time. The onus is then on you, on the reader, to be creative in how it is that you design movements to change the schools in your respective communities, that you seek out the reporters and journalists who you believe are sensitive to what you're discussing.

Those on the inside of media, like myself, make the comment "don't hate the media, become the media." And we try—I try. I can't do it, though, without your help, and you must be vigilant. You must be critical of the media. You must bring the grass roots here. You must take the grass roots into the newsrooms. You must present your case ceaselessly about why this is an American story that must be on the front page and displayed for what it is. Don't stop until you get that story in your paper, on your local radio station, on your national network news. It's your media. Take control of it.

INCARCERATED AND DISAPPEARED IN THE LAND OF THE FREE

by Trinh Minh-ha

World-renowned filmmaker and cultural theorist, Trinh Minh-ha, considers how America's urban crisis can be examined in the broader contexts of identity politics, both nationally and globally, and in the aftermath of legal policies produced as a consequence of the previous Bush/Cheney administration's war on terror, which continue to exert influence in civic and social dimensions to the present day. In Detroit and its bordering suburbs (especially the city of Dearborn, which combined with Detroit, hosts the largest Arab population outside of the Middle East), the effects of post-9/11 legal policies have been particularly acute, inflaming (as our contributor James Zogby notes in Chapter 4) already existing social tensions between respective racial populations (white, black, Latino) and Arab communities, as well as promoting a culture of fear of Islamic religious practices, or what has been defined as "Islamaphobia."[15]

Minh-ha argues that the war on terror abroad has had detrimental effects on U.S. democracy and efforts to address a broad spectrum of social and urban inequalities. A key focus of her essay concerns how well-documented practices of racial profiling in the United States have been influenced by the war on terror and extended to issues of immigration, nationality, culture, and gender, wherein unassimilated differences in American identity are viewed as a deviant, if not pathological, "Other" (as Houston Baker also identified) (e.g., undocumented Latinos are "illegal aliens," swine flu is a result of unchecked immigration, etc.). Minh-ha calls for no less than an educational praxis that will respond to these phobic constructions of identity and give rise to progressive forms of racial consciousness.

Reprinted with permission from *Elsewhere, Within Here: Immigration, Refugeeism and the Boundary Event* (New York and London: Routledge, 2010–2011).

In this brief intervention, I'll be focusing on the dynamics between the seen and the unseen, and on multiculturalism as being world mediated. There has been a time in the sixties, for example, when revolutionary leadership can with good conscience endeavor to open people's eyes and cure them from their blindness. But today, when opposites meet in the same rhetoric of Good and Evil, and bringing the invisible into visibility is no longer a simple one-way task, it seems more adequate to acknowledge that one is often blind, even with one's eyes open—until one learns to see, even with eyes wide shut.

Illiteracy, incarceration, segregation, unemployment, poverty, homicide and infanticide, as well as misogyny, rape and child abuse. The multifaceted problems we encounter in urban centers across the nation tell us with poignancy something about ourselves, about the system in which we participate, and about the irrevocable process of globalization. It is no accident that America with its incarceration rate has also proven to be the world's most aggressive jailer. And, it is no accident that Detroit, one of the largest cities in the nation, a city well known for its sustained protests and rebellions in the 40's and 60's, should also be among those struggling the hardest with illiteracy and unemployment. In a context where almost 70 percent of Metro Detroit students attend schools that are either 90 percent black or 90 percent white, one cannot help but notice how external and internal divisions of the State and the cities pass into one another in mutual reflection and reiteration.

We live with the remnants of a mind-set fixed on material evidence and accumulation, and on social structures built to separate, divide and conquer. With this in mind, it is hardly surprising that an educational system functioning as the pillar of these structures should become the enemy of certain youth groups; and literacy, no more, no less than a means to maintain them in line and promote conformity. As we face today's complex world networks of communication and dis-information in which logic is processed and language computerized, we are bound at times to question the validity of literacy—the assimilation into a dehumanizing machine so impoverished in spirit and imagination as to promote profit as *the* sole measure of value and economic growth as *the* sole measure of progress. Advanced technology can turn many of us, literate, into refugees; it can program us into conformity to the logic of a war machine that places numbers, quotas and the market well above the person.

Disfranchised groups continue to be treated as irregular cases—in which are marginal, abnormal and "other" all those individuals who deviate from the norms of a "good" and "just" society. As proven by practices fed into and disseminated by the media, these individuals are primarily (news) items; items to be quoted, traded and exploited in the system of commodified diversity. They are, by the same token, easily lumped together when the need to give a face to an invisible culprit calls for specific strategies of profiling. The targeting of neighborhoods for example, feeds on the logic that "They are all criminals who *look like* one" and *live there* where a greater crime rate is to be found. What is generated from inside the very core of a structure is deceptively isolated, displaced as outside society and dealt with as an alien element that needs conversion in order to be integrated. Evil is presented as coming from elsewhere and all that is needed to make it disappear is a precise cosmetic surgery with advanced technology. So goes the logic, and surely enough, what applies on the local and national scale inevitably applies on the global scale with U.S. foreign policy and warfare.

The dynamics of multiculturalism is world mediated. The war on terrorism has crystallized many of our phobias and prejudices. It gives racial profiling a new twist, while highlighting issues of immigration, identification, nationalization, as well as cultural and gender discrimination. There is a link between the way we define our elusive enemy abroad and the way we deal with our "others" at home, and certainly, there is a deep link between the way we identify our enemy and the way we define ourselves. We are being called upon to believe that we can eradicate terrorism by detaining and cross-examining outsiders in our midst. Such an attempt to define who's inside and who's outside in a society as heterogeneous as ours not only widens the divide between Americans and the world—the West and the Rest—but it also shows further conflicts among the multiple diverse fractions of our society. It has led to what a number of lawyers across the nation see as a dramatic constitutional crisis in U.S. history.

Blanket detentions, random searches, racial profiling and arbitrary prosecution of those who look suspect to our eyes are some of the solutions that have been adopted to give a visible front to what terrifies us. The enemy here is likely to be anyone who triggers the deep layers of our fear for the unexpected, the unknown, the abnormal, the foreign, in short, otherness as death. Each apparatus creates its own antibodies and its own enemies from within, and if blackness is equated with destruction in Detroit, on the world map, Africa is associated with AIDS, South America with drugs, Islam with terrorism, and the Third World with debt. The application of different standards to different people, the attack on suspicious-looking members of our society, their secret and indefinite confinement, have led to an oddly regressive social phenomenon: that of the disappeared in the land of the free.

An eye for an eye and the world goes blind, as peace activists have reminded us. Behind the appearance of socialization, integration and participation, policies are set up that de-socialize, disenfranchise and alienate whole communities. Sophisticated technology, clever economic exchange and exploitation (corporate robbery in our country, deceptive foreign aid, investment and free trade in the Third World are a few examples among many) dominate the social order, turning other sectors into dumping grounds or deserted zones for the poor and the rebel. With this in mind, the urgent task, as I see it, would be to bring to continual practice the critical role of civil society in "democratizing democracy."

For educators like ourselves, such a commitment to freedom rather than to domination and submission in education would entail a constant questioning of our relationship to knowledge, to the way we reserve, transmit or bring it to bear on our daily activities. Our ongoing critical view of the system is motivated, not by a mere desire to blame, to right the wrongs and to oppose for opposition's sake. Rather, it is motivated by the necessity to keep power and knowledge (ours and theirs) constantly in check for our own survival.

Considering the struggle that women of such groups as the So Sad in Detroit have been carrying on against child homicide and violent crime, the recent agreement of the Justice Department and Detroit to call in a monitor to oversee reform at the Police Department after years of complaints of misconduct is, hopefully, not a small step up in critical intervention and joint responsibility for social change. As a woman from an office of Save Our Sons and Daughters in the city put it, "We had 9/11 before 9/11. . . . We have it going on every day."

To say this, however, is also to say that the times of great difficulties are also the most enriching times. Ours is a time of change, of learning, of gaining wisdom and internal strength. A time when educators, artists, activists and other path makers are reminded that color, class, gender and culture are not categories, but an ongoing project and a dimension of consciousness. The capacity to transform ourselves and others in the very instance of our daily performances lies in the ability to expand our views and to create new, unexpected relationships among things, events and people. An educational praxis committed to changes both in the literate and the illiterate spheres should, among others, offer the possibility of a radical self-awareness in which words, speech and language are not just an exercise of power or resistance but also an infinite act of creativity.

NOTES

1. See, for example, Woody Doane, "Rethinking Whiteness Studies"; Margaret L. Andersen, "Whitewashing Race: A Critical Perspective on Whiteness"; Charles W. Mills, "White Supremacy as Sociopolitical System: A Philosophical Perspective"; and Eduardo Bonilla-Silva, "'New Racism,' Color-blind Racism, and the Future of Race in America," in *White Out: The Continuing Significance of Racism*, edited by Ashley "Woody" Doane and Eduardo Bonilla-Silva (New York: Routledge, 2003).

2. Michael Omi and Howard Winant argue that this critical approach is key to understanding structural and social functions of race, in *Racial Formation in the United States: From the 1960s to the 1990s* (New York: Routledge, 1994), pp. 54–55. We would also add that efforts to reclaim the language of race from its color-blind appropriation also require such critical methodology.

3. Bonilla-Silva's concept here can also be related to familiar analyses of the so-called postracial era, where matters of race have shifted from collective interests (as was the case during the 1960s civil rights movement) to individual interests, where race is primarily conceived in personal (i.e., nonstructural) terms (*Racism Without Racists: Color-Blind Racism and the Persistence of Racial Inequality in the United States*, New York: Rowman & Littlefield, 2006, pp. 1–24).

4. Bonilla-Silva, *Racism Without Racists*, pp. 12–23. A more recent survey in 2006 focusing on racial attitudes and affirmative action in metro Detroit was conducted by the Kirwan Institute for the Study of Race and Ethnicity and provides more data here.

5. john powell and Andrew Grant-Thomas provide an excellent definition and overview of racial framing in "Talking About Race: Toward a Transformative Agenda: Resource Notebook," their working paper prepared for the Kirwan Institute for the Study of Race and Ethnicity, August 2009, pp. 5–14.

6. Arizona's recent and inescapably racist anti-immigration law is a sobering example here, as only non-whites—and primarily Latinos—are viable subjects to its legal enforcement. Similarly, Arizona's recent efforts to ban race and ethnic studies classes in public education via its Ethnic Studies Law, as many critics have noted, primarily targets Latino and non-white populations. See, for example, Jonathan J. Cooper's, "Arizona Ethnic Studies Law Signed By Governor Brewer, Condemned By UN Human Rights Experts," in the *Huffington Post*, May 11, 2010.

7. We can find no other persuasive cause to explain this racial inequality except through the operations of structural racism.

8. Editors' note: The proposal did not pass in California, but a similar measure, endorsed by Connerly, did pass in Michigan, in 2006.

9. From the *New York Times*, © [January 7, 1996] The New York Times. All rights reserved. Used by permission and protected by the Copyright Laws of the United States. The printing, copying, redistribution, or retransmission of the Material, without express written permission, is prohibited.

10. Our reference here suggests the role semiotic theory, specifically as it is applied to the study of race and representation, can contribute to sociological studies of color-blind ideology. See, for example, Josh Bassett and Erica Frankenberg's "Parents Involved in Community Schools v. Seattle School District: A Social Science and Semiotic Analysis," their unpublished essay prepared for the Kirwan Institute for the Study of Race and Ethnicity's Kirwan Transformative Race Conference, Columbus, Ohio, November 30–December 2, 2007.

11. See Benjamin DeMott's *The Trouble with Friendship: Why Americans Can't Think Straight About Race* (New Haven, Ct.: Yale University Press, 1998). We would note our good fortune and privilege of working, however briefly, with Professor DeMott before his recent passing.

12. Tim Wise offers an excellent summation of this view in his book, *Between Barack and a Hard Place: Racism and White Denial in the Age of Obama* (San Francisco: City Lights Books, 2009). A noteworthy example here is to be found in The *Wall Street Journal*, which, the day after Barack Obama's election as president of the United States, declared that "Mr. Obama ha[d] a special obligation to help . . . put to rest the myth of racism as a barrier to achievement in this splendid country" (November 5, 2008, p. A 22).

13. Omi and Winant, *Racial Formation in the United States*, pp. 14–23. They analyze the fallacy of these arguments in their critique of the "ethnicity paradigm" of race.

14. Omi and Winant, *Racial Formation in the United States*, pp. 73–76.

15. Our specific application of the term here applies to intolerance.

3

MASS INCARCERATION
and the Urban Crisis

One of the most critical, but often unexamined,[1] structural/ institutional forces sustaining America's urban crisis is what has long been identified in the fields of sociology and criminal justice as the practice of "mass incarceration."[2] This practice emerged in the 1970s under the Nixon administration's and in the 1980s under the Reagan administration's war on drugs[3] and has had the dubious impact of transforming America into the world's largest jailer, with more than two million people currently under incarceration. The costs and consequences of maintaining such an historically unprecedented number of people behind bars—or what our contributor, Marc Mauer, defines as the establishment of "a permanent state of mass incarceration,"[4]—has been detrimental to the United States across a wide spectrum of social and economic indices but has most acutely affected primarily urban black and Latino communities, who, while comprising approximately 25 percent of the nation's population, account for more than 60 percent of its prisoners. This glaring racial inequality is even more significant when one considers that on average *all* black males in the United States have about a 32 percent chance of being imprisoned; followed by Latino males, at 17 percent; and white males, who despite making up approximately 32 percent of the U.S. population, have a 6 percent chance of incarceration.[5]

It must also be noted that now a record number of women are in U.S. prisons and that the increase in their percentage rate of incarceration is approaching levels twice that of males.[6]

Economically, the total financial costs of the U.S. prison system, via local, state, and federal expenditures, exceed $200 billion annually,[7] with Michigan accounting for $2 billion a year (or 20 percent of its general fund), a figure that means Michigan now spends nearly 20 percent more per dollar on its prison systems than on funding for public universities and community colleges.[8]

The practice of mass incarceration—which Mauer indicates marks a substantial departure from a forty-year period, from the 1920s to the 1960s, in which the U.S. prison population remained remarkably stable at about 200,000 incarcerated[9]—has also transformed the traditional status of the prison from a civic institution into a private industry that generates economic benefits to a network of business interests and predominantly rural geographies across the United States, where such prisons are often located. The result of this has been the creation of what analysts in the last decade have defined as the "prison-industrial complex."[10] Noted scholar and activist Angela Davis has written extensively on the prison-industrial complex[11] and has described it as a nationwide civic and institutional apparatus that has mobilized police and "prisons as a failed 'solution' to social, political, and economic problems"[12] that are foundational to urban crisis conditions.

Though a comprehensive discussion of the operations and impact of the prison-industrial complex is beyond the scope of this chapter, three key areas will be addressed: (1) the relationship between color-blind ideology and the dynamics of racial inequalities within the U.S. criminal justice system, (2) the collateral consequences of mass incarceration on urban communities in terms of civic engagement (e.g., voting rights, political representation, etc.) and identity politics, and (3) the role of education in terms of rehabilitation and social reentry programs for the formerly incarcerated.

MASS INCARCERATION, CIVIL DEATH, AND THE NEW RACIAL DOMAIN

by Manning Marable

Manning Marable's analysis offers an important overview of historical events and political policies during the last several decades that have contributed to the crisis of mass incarceration in the U.S. criminal justice system. He references the work of sociologist Lawrence Bobo and his analysis of "laissez-faire racism"[13] to argue that color-blind discourse has promoted the widespread social belief that racialized structures of inequality in education, employment, and criminal justice practices themselves (e.g., disproportionate punishments oriented by race) have little or no relevant influence on the vast disproportion of black and Latino populations who are currently incarcerated in the United States. Instead, Marable argues, the perception is that crime is severed from any structural context and reduced to a matter of individual behavior. This view influences broader social perceptions of racial identity, including promoting pathological views of black and Latino culture, which we will argue, in this context, have the effect of suggesting that there is a racial/biological component to crime (e.g., "If blacks/Latinos move into white neighborhoods, crime will increase, property values will decline," etc.). As noted, such views, of course, can be related to now discredited theories of scientific racism that were especially prevalent during the nineteenth century.

Marable also importantly discusses his own original concepts of "civil death" and the "new racial domain" that he theorizes have been produced by the operations of mass incarceration and its direct and collateral effects on U.S. populations.

We possess the issue before us of rebuilding lives, which, in turn, implies that social, economic, and political pressures have unfairly restricted or destroyed genuine opportunities and aspirations of millions of people. The challenge before us is not just to rebuild shattered lives, but to restore individuals from civil society's margins back to the center. Our challenge is to understand and comprehend the destructive structural processes of marginalization and exploitation in order to transform them.

One of the greatest structural barriers to human development in U.S. history has, of course, been the barrier of racism. It is a barrier that American society has not yet overcome. What do scholars in the social sciences talk about when they talk about structural racism today? After all, the white and colored signs that were ubiquitous throughout the Jim Crow South have long since disappeared. Legal racial segregation in the United States was outlawed more than a generation ago. However, scholars such as sociologist Larry Bobo have argued that the traditional color line in American life has not vanished but has merely been reconfigured. Bobo writes that the death of Jim Crow racism has left us in an uncomfortable place called the state of laissez-faire racism. He describes laissez-faire racism as a situation where society has ideals, but openness to very limited amounts of integration at the personal level remains.

Political stagnation exists regarding some types of affirmative action, quite negative stereotypes of racial minorities persist, and a wide gulf in perceptions regarding the importance of racial discrimination remains. Many middle-class blacks and Latinos today accept the national political narrative about the pluralistic promise of American democracy, that through individual initiative and personal responsibility, we can teach our children success and upward mobility. They believe that our institutions of law and order are race-neutral and color-blind. They are taught and believe that the processes of adjudicating justice do not have to be color coded into unequal and unfair hierarchies. The fundamental problem with that perspective is that laissez faire racism is still racism, albeit less overt and articulated in a race-neutral language of fairness. The continuing existence of racialized inequality can be measured by social scientists, such as myself, in very specific social outcomes that are not a product of the lack of individual initiative but inequality that is the product of deep structural barriers that continue to be maintained through the pervasive power of white privilege. Racialized inequality presents itself in the post–civil rights era as a normal aspect of the general social fabric of U.S. society. In other words, in the post–civil rights era, there are winners and losers in the competition for resources and power in our United States. The implication is that if Latinos and African Americans find themselves at the lower end of society's totem pole and disproportionately represented inside the nation's correctional facilities, the overwhelming logic of the commonsense color-blind racism of the twenty-first century is that we only have ourselves to blame. The modern assault against racial fairness and against the principle of equality in America has been over the last ten to fifteen years, in the post–civil rights era, simultaneously political, economic, cultural, and ideological.

In the eighties and nineties, there was a dedicated concerted effort by conservatives to literally turn the discourse of the civil rights movement upside down, in effect to rewrite the American public's memory of what actually transpired in the fifties and sixties. Dr. Martin Luther King's image and words were cynically manipulated to provide a posthumous endorsement for outlawing affirmative action programs. An important turning point occurred in California, in November 1996, with the passage of Proposition 209—the so-called civil rights initiative. Winning by a margin of 54 to 46 percent, the initiative outlawed the use of race, sex, color, ethnicity, or national origin in many aspects of public life. Thousands of black and Latino voters, confused by the language of the initiative, failed to understand that affirmative action would be outlawed in California and actually voted for it. On the day of the referendum, *Los Angeles Times* exit polls indicated that a clear majority of California voters supported affirmative action programs, yet these very same voters, confused or not, approved Proposition 209 and made it the state law.

All of this was made possible because the lessons in history of the civil rights movement have largely been erased from the national consciousness. We are so far from the struggle against desegregation, so far from the legal battles of the *Brown* decision, so far removed from the marches at Selma and Birmingham and Montgomery that somehow the generation who did not march has forgotten how to march. White moderates and liberals who long defended race-based affirmative action programs waffled and largely collapsed before this conservative onslaught. Setting the tone was President Clinton himself, who in his reelection campaign of 1996, even declared that he had "done more to eliminate affirmative action programs I didn't think were fair and tightened up others than my predecessors have done since affirmative action has been around."

Clinton's failure to frame the continuing necessity and the argument for affirmative action around issues of compensatory justice within the historic framework of the struggle against racialized injustice in the United States and the need to implement measures to address and compensate the oppressed for these deep patterns of racialized inequality would prove to be decisive when it came to issues of crime, punishment, and justice, which I'll deal with shortly. In 1996, the U.S. Court of Appeals for the Fifth Circuit and the *Hopwood v. the State of Texas* decision outlawed the use of race as a factor for admissions to universities. Initiative 200, in Washington State, in 1998, followed California in outlawing affirmative action enforcement as a direct consequence. In the first year of Proposition 209's enforcement, the number of African-American first-year undergraduates enrolling at the Berkeley campus of the University of California fell from 258 to 95. At the University of California at Los Angeles, the drop was 211 black students down to 125.

In June 2003, the U.S. Supreme Court decided two lawsuits involving affirmative action programs at the University of Michigan at Ann Arbor. The more important of these two decisions, *Gratz v. Bollinger et al.*, declared that there was indeed a compelling state interest in fostering programs enhancing diversity and that the quality of education was indeed enriched by having individuals from different racial and ethnic backgrounds as part of the university environment. Therefore, the court declared in its narrow five to four ruling, the use of race as a factor was indeed acceptable so long as it was not applied as a quota. In effect, the Lewis Powell standard set by the *Bakke* decision of 1978 was still deemed constitutional.

We all collectively breathed a sigh of relief. The initial response from the academic community and the civil rights community was that it represented a great victory. Did it? We unfortunately ignored the full weight of the majority's opinion on the high court that universities had to consider henceforth prospective students as individuals and not to reject or admit through any programs based primarily or exclusively on what was perceived to be racial categories.

This part of the ruling was quickly interpreted to mean that all programs, no matter how large or small, of any college should not be based primarily or exclusively, or seen to be based, on anything that smacked of racial categories. Because of this interpretation, we have seen hundreds and hundreds of colleges and universities wiping out minority-oriented programs designed to address the historic gap—the lack of access to higher education of blacks and Latinos, which is a product of a racialized history of inequality in having equitable access to advanced learning in this country. It was not based on the lack of individual initiative by blacks or Latinos to desire a higher education. It was based on structural barriers that kept us out. Now, all of these programs are under the gun and being wiped away. This is the racialized context of the assault—the dismantling of affirmative action and programs of compensatory justice. I will use this as a segue for our discussion about what is occurring inside of the racialized criminal justice system. The system of Jim Crow segregation may have indeed disappeared legally, but in its place has emerged what I call in my writing the new racial domain—the NRD.

This new racial domain of color-blind racism of the twenty-first century is a complex reconfiguration of race, prejudice, and power in the context of a political economy of neo-liberalism and globalization. I would implore that you do not discuss criminal justice in a political and economic vacuum. Understand the context in which justice is being allocated within a framework of an increasingly global capitalist economy, within the context of millions of jobs being exported overseas, within a context of structural unemployment, where millions and millions of Americans are trapped in lower-paying jobs and pushed out of the economy.

One cannot talk about a process of criminal justice without looking at it in the context of the economy in which it exists. This new racial domain is a deadly triangle or perhaps, for those in the faith community, an unholy trinity of structural racism. The unholy trinity that we are combating is mass unemployment, mass incarceration, and mass disenfranchisement. Mass unemployment, mass incarceration, and mass disenfranchisement—it is on those three elements that the color-blind racism of the twenty-first century of the new racial domain has been constructed right before our very eyes, leading to marginalization in the economy, stigmatization of the individual, and social exclusion because of the liabilities imposed by a felony conviction, culminating potentially into what could be called civil death—the absence of a capacity to engage in civil society.

The cycle of destruction starts with chronic mass unemployment and poverty. Real incomes for the majority of working poor people actually fell during Clinton's second term in office. After the 1996 Welfare Act, the social safety net was largely pulled apart.

As the Bush administration took power, chronic joblessness spread like wildfire but particularly to black workers in the manufacturing sector. By early 2004, in cities such as New York, fully one-half of all black male adults were outside of the paid labor force. Mass unemployment of that type inevitably breeds mass incarceration. About one-third of all prisoners were unemployed at the time of their arrest. Others averaged less than $20,000 annual income in the year prior to their arrest. When the Attica prison uprising occurred in upstate New York in 1971, there were only 12,500 prisoners in New York State's correctional facilities. There were nationwide about 300,000 prisoners. By the year 2001, New York State held over 71,000 women and men in its prisons.

Nationwide, over two million women and men are incarcerated today. Today, about five million Americans are arrested annually. Nearly one in five Americans now possesses a criminal record, and that's not just blacks and Latinos. One in five—nearly one in five—possesses a criminal record. You cannot arrest millions and millions of people and not have it impact white America as well. Mandatory minimum sentencing laws, adopted in the 1980s and the early 1990s in many states, stripped judges of their discretionary powers in sentencing—imposing draconian terms on first-time and nonviolent offenders. Parole has been made much more restrictive as well.

In 1995, Pell grant subsidies supporting educational programs for prisoners were ended. For those fortunate enough to be successful in navigating the criminal justice bureaucracy and emerging from incarceration, they discovered that both federal and state governments explicitly prohibit the employment of convicted ex-felons in literally hundreds of vocations. And so the cycle of unemployment frequently starts the deadly triad—the deadly trinity again. In seven states, former prisoners convicted of a felony lose the right to vote, for life.

What are the economic costs for U.S. society of this vast expansion of what scholars now routinely refer to as the prison-industrial complex? According to criminal justice researcher David Barlow, at the University of Wisconsin at Milwaukee, between 1980 and 2000, the combined expenditures for federal, state, and local government on police increased about 400 percent. Corrections expenditures for building new prisons, upgrading existing facilities, hiring more prison guards, and related costs increased about 1,000 percent in twenty years—1,000 percent! Although it cost about $70,000 in 2001 dollars to construct a typical prison cell and about $25,000 annually to supervise and maintain each prisoner, the United States still was and is building hundreds of new prison cells in this country every week. If you build it, they reason, they must come.

The greatest victims of these racialized processes, those for whom they are building these new prison cells, are, of course, Latinos and African Americans and especially our young women and men. In April 2000, utilizing national and state data compiled by the FBI, the Justice Department and six leading foundations issued a comprehensive study, documenting the vast racial disparities at every level of the juvenile justice process. African Americans under the age of eighteen comprise 15 percent of their national age group, yet they represented 26 percent of all those who were arrested.

After entering the criminal justice system, black and white juveniles with identical records are treated in radically different ways. According to the Justice Department study, among white youth offenders, 66 percent were referred to juvenile courts, while only 31 percent of African-American youth were taken there. Blacks comprised 44 percent of those detained in juvenile jails, 46 percent of all those tried in adult criminal courts, and 58 percent of all juveniles who were warehoused in adult prisons. Now, in practical terms, this means that for young African Americans who are arrested and charged with a crime, they are more than six times more likely to be assigned to prison than white youthful offenders.

For young people who have never been to prison before, African Americans are nine times more likely than whites to be sentenced to juvenile prisons. For youths charged with a drug offense, blacks are forty-eight times more likely than whites to be sentenced to juvenile correctional facilities. That's forty-eight times more likely. This is not an accident. Statistically, it is impossible for that to be an accident. Once black and brown women and men are ensnared in this system, they routinely experience the same kind of racial profiling in our courts. According to studies of the U.S. Commission on Civil Rights, black Americans constitute 15 percent of the nation's drug users. Why is it then that we comprise one-third of all those arrested for drug charges? Why is it that we comprise over half of those convicted on drug charges? Why is it that we comprise 70 percent of all Americans imprisoned on drug charges—15 percent, 33 percent, 50 percent. Something must be wrong with the math, or something must be racialized in the criminal justice system.

What are the political consequences for regulating black, brown, and poor people through the criminal justice and penal systems? Perhaps the greatest impact is on the process of voting and disenfranchisement. According to an October 1998 study, "Losing the Vote"—produced by the Sentencing Project and the Human Rights Watch, two nonprofit research groups—using 1998 figures, 4.5 million Americans, or one out of every 50 adults, had been currently losing or had permanently lost the ability to vote because of a felony conviction. At that time, in thirty-two states, convicted offenders were not permitted to vote while on parole. In ten states, former prisoners who had fully served their terms remained disenfranchised. In many of those states, ex-felons were prohibited from voting for the rest of their lives.

For African Americans, these figures were translated in the 1996 presidential election to 4.6 million black males who could vote and did vote but 1.4 million black men who were denied the right to vote. Even though they paid taxes and are citizens of this country, they were disenfranchised. The racial disenfranchisement of black people is absolutely stunning and can only be understood as rolling back the structural gains of the civil rights movement.

In Florida, 31 percent of all black males have been permanently disenfranchised. In five other states—Iowa, Mississippi, New Mexico, Virginia, and Wyoming—one in four black males is permanently disenfranchised. In Delaware, one in five black males—20 percent—is permanently barred from voting. In Texas, one in five black males is currently disenfranchised. In four states—Minnesota, New Jersey, Rhode Island, and Wisconsin—between 16 and 18 percent of all black males are currently disenfranchised. In nine states—Arizona, Connecticut, Georgia, Maryland, Missouri, Nebraska, Nevada, Oklahoma, and Tennessee—between 10 and 15 percent of all black males are currently disenfranchised.

What does it all mean to us? In effect, what it means is that the Voting Rights Act of 1965—which guaranteed on paper that we were equal citizens, which guaranteed on paper that we were participants in American democracy—has been repealed by state restrictions on former prisoners, a people who are imprisoned in racialized processes that are inherently discriminatory. These are not Marable's statistics. These are the FBI's, the U.S. Justice Department's statistics. When an entire group of people experience racialized injustice at the bar of justice, when they serve their time and come out and then continue to be barred, in many cases, for the rest of their natural life, I don't know what you call that political system, but you sure shouldn't call it a democracy.

Some of my colleagues in higher education (and I'll pick on my own university, Columbia) politely tell me when they hear me talk about the new racial domain or mass incarceration that they have guilt fatigue. They are implying that blacks complain too much and that they aren't guilty, that is, white upper-middle-class males aren't guilty of oppressing anybody. They didn't enslave anybody. They didn't put anybody in jail. They didn't support mandatory minimums. They thought it was a bad idea. Why should they bear the burden of the cost of addressing these obvious inequalities that still exist within the racialized criminal justice system? Well, first, there is a crucial difference between guilt and responsibility. White Americans who are alive today are not guilty of enslaving anybody in the legal definition of the term. Most white Americans below the age of fifty played no direct role supporting—actively supporting—Jim Crow segregation. They are not guilty of overt acts to block integration of public accommodations and public schools.

But white Americans, as a group, continue to be the direct beneficiaries of the legal apparatuses of white supremacy in this country, carried out by the full weight of America's legal, political, and economic institutions. The consequences of state-sponsored racialized inequality create a mountain of historically constructed accumulated disadvantage that cannot simply be swept away by saying "I'm not responsible." The living legacy of that racialized accumulated disadvantage can easily be measured by looking at the gross racial inequalities that continue to segment Americans by race in their life expectancies, and in their unequal access to home ownership, business development, and quality education.

The U.S. government for nearly two centuries established the legal parameters for corporations to carry out blatantly discriminatory practices and policies. Consequently, it is insufficient for us to simply say that once segregation laws were changed and wiped off the books, the government's responsibility to address those victimized by three centuries of legal discriminatory public policies has therefore ended. The U.S. government and various state governments created and perpetuated legal racial disparities. They are indeed responsible for compensating the victims and their descendants. As citizens of this country, we all must bear our share of the financial burden for the crimes against humanity, carried out by our own government. In short, there must be a rendezvous with America's racial history. There must be a rendezvous with the new racial domain for black, brown, and white alike if democracy, if freedom, is to mean anything in the twenty-first century.

What should that rendezvous look like? What is the long-term national impact for destroying the lives of millions of brown and black young women and men in this country? How does it affect the white majority—soon to be, by the mid-twenty-first century, our largest minority group? We foster the illusion of safety and security but not its reality. We spent $150 billion in the past year to pursue a war against terrorism by invading Iraq, where we discovered not a single weapon of mass destruction. Yet, for all of the Bush Administration's rhetoric about homeland security, our neighborhoods are increasingly less safe and less secure.

In 2004, because of budget reductions, we saw all over the country large numbers of police and corrections personnel laid off. Cleveland laid off 250 police officers—15 percent of its total police force. In Los Angeles County, the sheriff's department fired 1,200 deputies and, due to budget cuts, was forced to close several county corrections facilities. In Pittsburgh, one-quarter of its entire police force was cut. In Houston, 190 corrections officers in the city jail were let go and replaced by Houston police officers. Innovative law enforcement projects that were effective in reducing homicide rates and street crime in our neighborhoods in the nineties are being scaled back and, in some cases, eliminated entirely. So, in our neighborhoods, we are less safe, regardless of whether Osama bin Laden is caught or not.

We're spending $150 billion abroad and cutting back domestic security at home. What sense does that make? What is responsible for this? What is responsible for destroying the lives of millions of young Americans of color? That is really the central question you must ask today. The national security state—the pursuit of permanent war abroad in the new racial domain and the prison-industrial complex at home—severely reduces resources available for everything else for human needs, for investment in human capital. One of the best examples of this is higher education. According to the National Conference of State Legislatures, in fiscal year 2004, New York State reduced its general fund appropriations for higher education by 2.5 percent. In Texas, in fiscal year 2004, the reduction was 5.5 percent. California's was a staggering 8.9 percent. Nationwide, the reduction was 2.6 percent in fiscal year 2004, with nearly half of all states reducing higher education expenditures. In Michigan, state education spending in fiscal year 2004, compared to 2003, dropped 6.2 percent; in Colorado, 13.7 percent; and in Massachusetts, 21.8 percent. Those who are shortchanged are overwhelmingly and disproportionately black, brown, working class, and poor.

The new oppressions of the racial domain demand the construction of a new civil rights movement. I say "a new movement," because it is not simply walking across the Edmund Pettus Bridge in Selma on our way to Montgomery. I say "a new movement," because it is not simply trying to get a cup of coffee at a lunch counter in Greensboro, North Carolina. I say "a new movement," because of the political economy of mass incarceration and how it generates profits for some and human misery for millions. I say "a new movement," because in upstate New York, 80,000 jobs are generated by those prisons, which is why, between 1817 and 1981, New York State built thirty-three prisons, but in the twenty years after 1981 to 2001, they built thirty-eight state prisons. Prisons create jobs—jobs at our expense.

On top of that, the prisoner population is counted in the population of that region regarding state apportionment of the members of the state legislature. So, in states like New York, three to four state legislative districts are, in effect, prison districts. This is about politics. Over 90 percent of all the prisoners in New York State are in prisons that, just coincidentally, are in Republican state senatorial districts. Republican districts benefit. Perhaps that's just a coincidence—but perhaps not.

We need a new civil rights movement. We need the reconstruction of democracy, where all voices, all members of society, can finally be at the decision-making table. The new civil rights movement will require legislative initiatives at local, state, and national levels. It will require faith-based institutions, churches, synagogues, and mosques to mobilize their members to embrace the concept that public safety and personal security are directly linked to the reintegration and restoration of civic rights and opportunities for the millions of Americans stigmatized by felony convictions. This is a battle we must win. Our goals must be restorative justice and civic capacity building—to bring back from the margins millions of Americans routinely denied jobs due to prior felony convictions; to bring back into our political voting process the millions of American citizens who are unfairly stigmatized and excluded from exercising their constitutional democratic right to vote; to bring back ex-prisoners into our economy by challenging and eliminating the state-sanctioned lists of specific jobs that former prisoners are unfairly denied access to even though they are fully qualified; and by civic engagement, to bring back from unemployment into the economic mainstream the latent leadership, creativity, and talent of millions of people who have been victimized by the new racial domain.

We can insist on reforms within our legal system that treat all juveniles, regardless of their race, with equal respect, with equal fairness under the law. We can insist on it, and we must win this battle for our children. We can demand the infusion of constructive, meaningful educational programs inside our prisons and the availability and restoration of Pell grant program assistance to provide bridges of learning for hundreds of thousands of incarcerated women and men. We know scientifically that prisoners who have access to college educational programming have a recidivism rate of barely 10 percent. Those who do not have access to those programs return to prisons at rates anywhere from 40 to 70 percent. We know it makes sense to invest small amounts to educate incarcerated young women and men so they don't return to prison. Let us use our money wisely. We can implement restorative justice programs focusing on therapeutic jurisprudence and rehabilitative programs, constructive and creative alternatives, redirecting hundreds of thousands of nonviolent offenders and first-time felony offenders out of the dead end of maximum security penal institutions.

I regularly lecture in Sing Sing prison. Sing Sing is a maximum security prison, notorious in American history. Forty-four percent of the prisoners in Sing Sing are nonviolent drug offenders. They don't belong in Sing Sing. They have a public health problem; they don't have a maximum security problem. It is unconscionable and immoral for nonviolent offenders to be placed in maximum security in the context of a system that creates criminalization. You have to face facts. Every year, 600,000 of the two million people incarcerated get out. Coming out of prison, young brothers and sisters are not the same people who went in. What are we doing to our families, the thousands of cases of spousal abuse, the hundreds of thousands of children placed into foster care? What are the implications for the destruction of broken families and households and lives through the new racial domain? We need a civil rights movement to heal and redeem ourselves as a people.

To conclude, in our neighborhoods, we can demand new funds to implement and to sustain constructive, nonconfrontational policing approaches to most of our problems of local crime. In cities like Detroit, the effects of the fiscal crisis of the national security state—the spending of billions on a permanent military—mean underfunding for nearly everything else, and I'll just focus on one issue, our public schools. Closing public health clinics, halting the construction of affordable, publicly subsidized housing—all those are issues, but I'll just focus on the public school question.

Recently, Detroit officials projected that between twenty-five and forty public schools may close due to budget cuts.[14] As many as 4,000 staff jobs may be eliminated. How many thousands of young people's lives will be negatively affected by our state and national obsession to place human needs last in our fiscal and public policy priorities?

But this unholy trinity—mass incarceration, mass disenfranchisement, and mass unemployment—of the new racial domain and its destructive processes can successfully be challenged and overturned. We do possess the power to change the way things are. We can fight for the restoration of voting rights for every American citizen, whether they have previously been incarcerated or not. It's a simple democratic principle. If you are a citizen or a permanent resident of this country, if you pay your taxes, you have earned the democratic and inalienable right to vote and to be heard in America.

Why should the conservative red-state, white upper-middle-class Americans listen to the voices of the new civil rights movement? Prosaically, I could say because Dr. King once said, "The moral ark of the universe is long but it bends toward justice." But, politically, I will tell you why they will have to listen. They will have to listen because, just like us, they can look at the demographics of this country and workplace projections. If the white population in the United States around 2016 peaks in size and if birthrates continue to decline to lower than 1.9 births per couple, the population will begin to decline. Hispanics, blacks, and Asian Pacific Island Americans, taken collectively, will outnumber non-Hispanic whites before mid-century. This is already happening all over the United States. It's already happened in California, and it's happened in most of our major cities today. Who's going to do the work? Black and brown people, increasingly, and that's reflected in the demographics of employment.

Our country is a pluralistic country. When you penalize black and brown young women and men, when you incarcerate them, when you strip them of the democratic right of voting, when you stigmatize them and keep them outside of civil society, how can you expect them to respect the law and political institutions? What kind of nonsense is that? Your best guarantee for security is investment in humanity—investment in human possibility. That is the best guarantor for a safe, secure, and civil democratic society. We all have a stake in this—black, white, and brown alike.

The great danger is that many white Americans who recognize that racialized inequalities continue and who acknowledge the existence of the new racial domain and the inherent unfairness of the criminal justice system will nevertheless fight to keep things the way they are. Much of the reactionary populism and the anti-immigrant bashing—from politicians such as Pat Buchanan—are motivated by a desire to maintain the old white privilege entitlements of being free, white, and twenty-one.

But there is another alternative—a multiracial democratic society, where all racial groups are stakeholders in a common civic project called democracy.

For several years, I have lectured at New York's Sing Sing prison as part of a master's degree program sponsored by the New York Theological Seminary. During one of my most recent visits, I noticed that the corrections officers had erected a large yellow sign over the door of a public entrance to the prison. The sign read: "Through these doors pass some of the finest corrections officers in the world."

I asked Reverend Bill Webber, the director of the prison's education program, and several prisoners what they thought about the sign. Bill answered bluntly, "Demonic . . . demonic." I immediately thought of the sign over Auschwitz: "Work makes us free." One of the master's students—a thirty-five-year-old Latino named Tony— agreed with Bill's assessment, but added, "Brother Manning, it is indeed demonic, but perhaps, let us face the demon head-on."

And so, my sisters and brothers, over two million of our fellow Americans are now incarcerated in this country. Millions of Americans who pay taxes, who are citizens of this country, and who work hard are barred from the one thing that defines American citizenship—the right to vote. We live in a country with five to six million Americans who cannot vote. One million Americans declared bankruptcy this year alone. Approximately 45 million Americans are without medical care. For the sake of our children, for the sake of all Americans who are ensnared and stigmatized by mass incarceration, mass disenfranchisement, and mass unemployment, it is time to face the demon head-on.

MASS INCARCERATION, RACE, AND CRIMINAL JUSTICE POLICY

by Marc Mauer

Mauer's commentary offers a brief synopsis of four major facets of the U.S. criminal justice system, which he examines comprehensively in his now classic text, Race to Incarcerate. *In that work, Mauer traces the evolution of the U.S. prison system from a "reactive model,"[15] which changed little over the course of nearly two centuries, to its contemporary transformation into an apparatus that, as noted, has established a state of mass incarceration within the nation. Mauer asserts that it is crucial to understand, within the context of mass incarceration, that actual crime rates in the United States have not appreciably changed during the last several decades. Rather, the exponential increase in prison populations is a consequence of policy changes, including mandatory sentencing policies, "three strikes" laws, and the continued prosecution of the war on drugs via imprisonment, as opposed to non-incarcerative recovery/rehabilitation programs. In considering the gross racial inequality of incarcerated populations, Mauer asserts that crime enforcement vis à vis the war on drugs primarily focuses on poor urban black and Latino communities. In addition to imprisonment, such crime enforcement has the consequence of promoting social views that such communities are prone to criminal behavior and thus expendable, a point he powerfully addresses in his book, when he states that there would be no complacency in responding to this crisis if white populations were so disproportionately incarcerated.[16] Indeed, Mauer calls for the development of a new criminal justice linguistic and policy framework, severed from any context of stereotypes of the criminal black and Latino male and oriented by the recognition that the majority of incarcerated populations in the United States are not irrevocably criminal but are people with ties to family and communities, who should have, where appropriate, an opportunity during all stages of incarceration to pursue contributing lives.*

What I'd like to try to do is to frame the experience of incarceration over the last several decades and to describe what I think are some of the lessons we can learn from this experience.

The growth in incarceration is a story that goes back to 1972, when the prison population began to rise in this country. Let's imagine we're back in 1972. Richard Nixon is president, and President Nixon comes on national television to make an address to the American people about the problem of crime, and here's what he says: "My fellow Americans, we have a serious problem of crime in this country, but I have a plan for dealing with it. Here's my plan. First, we'll build a million prison cells and fill them as quickly as possible. Second, because we know that crime takes place in minority communities, we'll reserve two-thirds of those prison cells for blacks and Latinos. And, third, we'll put 3,000 people on death row and start to execute them as quickly as possible. That's my plan for dealing with crime."

Now, what would have happened if he'd made such a speech? We would have seen major protests by civil rights organizations. Editorial writers of leading newspapers would have decried this barbaric plan for dealing with the problem of crime—building prisons, executing people.

Nixon never made such a speech, but this is precisely what our criminal justice policy has brought us over the last thirty years. We've indeed added more than a million people in the prison system. Including local jails, we have two million people behind bars. Indeed, nearly two-thirds of the people incarcerated are people of color. If we look on death row, we have more than 3,000 people awaiting execution. Almost 1,000 people have been executed over the last twenty-five years. The United States has become the world leader in incarceration. That's what our policies—our combined social and criminal justice policies—have led to.

There are four lessons we can learn from this.

First, the increase in incarceration is a result of a conscious change in policy, not increases in crime rate. What does this look like? Basically, a movement toward more determinant sentencing, taking discretion away from judges and corrections officials. It takes the form of mandatory sentencing, which exists in almost every state now, as well as policies like three strikes and you're out, which exist in about half the states.

The most extreme, of course, is in California—their three strikes policy. The policy was challenged in 2003 in the Supreme Court. One of the cases involved a man whose third strike was for stealing videotapes worth $153 from a K-Mart store. The Supreme Court found that the three strikes policy was not cruel and unusual, deferring to the judgment of the legislators in enacting such policies in the interest of public safety. That videotape thief is now doing fifty years to life in a California prison. That's what this policy has brought us.

Lesson number two is that the get-tough movement, in particular the war on drugs, has probably been the most significant factor contributing to this increase in incarceration. In 1980, about 40,000 people were in prison or jail for a drug offense. We've since had more than a tenfold increase to 500,000 people today, either awaiting trial or serving time for a drug offense. Even more so than for our prison policies overall, the racial dynamics are inescapable here. Two-thirds of the people in prison for a drug offense are African American or Latino.

We have a war on drugs that is essentially a two-tiered war. We know that drug use and drug abuse cut across class and race lines, but drug law enforcement is primarily focused in low-income communities of color. In well-off communities, when parents find out their kid has a drug problem, they don't call the cops; they call their friends who are social workers, and they find the best treatment program they can get. In low-income communities, we don't have those same kinds of resources. So, the problem becomes defined as a criminal justice problem, one that involves police, prosecutors, and prisons, and there's never any shortage of those kinds of resources.

Lesson number three is that if we presume that the prison buildup is supposed to control crime, it's had a relatively modest and diminishing impact in that regard. The decade of the 1990s was a period in which crime was going down across the country; many political leaders have been quick to take credit for this and say that locking people up in prison was the reason for that decline.

We don't know all the answers to this yet, but the research that's been done suggests that about a quarter of the decline in violent crime was a result of the increase in incarceration. Is that good news or bad news? A quarter of the decline is a significant number of crimes and a significant number of people who were not victimized as a result of this policy. But it also tells us that three-quarters of the decline had nothing to do with the prison buildup.

Therefore, what else was going on? The economy was relatively strong in the 1990s. More low-wage jobs were available to keep teenagers employed and out of trouble. There was the crack cocaine epidemic of the late eighties and early nineties, which had already reached its peak and was waning, as drug epidemics typically have done over the years. In some cities, the community policing also led to more strategic approaches that kept guns out of the hands of young people, and young people changing their behaviors as well.

Finally, the fourth lesson is that if we look at the effectiveness of prison, even assuming prison may have been responsible for a quarter of the decline in crime, this does not tell us whether this is the most effective way we could approach this problem. A good deal of research tells us that interventions with families at risk, preschool programs, and incentives to complete high school graduation, as well as substance abuse treatment, have all demonstrated they can be more cost effective than continued prison expansion.

So, the problem is not so much that we don't know what can work. The problem is more one of political will. We need to change a political climate where people in prison and their families are viewed as expendable, where they're viewed as the price we have to pay for changes in the broader economic and social structure. If we want to address these broad issues, we need to change the political climate so we can do what's right and what we know will actually work to promote public safety.

RACIAL PROFILING AND IMPRISON-MENT OF THE MENTALLY ILL[17]

by Bob Herbert

Bob Herbert, a columnist for the New York Times, *offers commentary on a series of articles he wrote for the* Times, *in the late summer of 1999, which, otherwise, initially received little national attention by mainstream media. The focus of his articles concerned the blanket arrest of approximately forty African Americans on false drug charges, in the small town of Tulia, Texas, by disgraced police officer Tom Coleman, who was awarded "Texas Lawman of the Year" for his efforts. Herbert cites this case as an example of why there needs to be a much more forceful address of the issue of innocent populations who are imprisoned, especially those who are subject to racial profiling. Another key area Herbert outlines is the fact that U.S. prisons now incarcerate substantial numbers of the mentally ill population, some 200,000 in 2008,[18] who do not belong in prison but are suffering the consequences of a failed nationwide mental health care system. Herbert also draws attention to the familiar links between the disproportionate percentage of unemployed urban populations and entry into the prison-industrial complex.*

When we talk about mass imprisonment, I think not nearly enough attention is given to the numbers of people who are in prison and absolutely shouldn't be there at all because they were innocent. I remember not too long ago I did about a dozen columns out of Tulia, Texas, where dozens of African Americans were rounded up in a drug sting went amuck—it was actually 10 percent of the black population of Tulia—and charged not just with drug possession or simply being a dealer but with being major drug dealers. No drugs were found in these arrests. No guns were found. No money was found.

I used to work for the *Daily News* in New York, and I tend to recognize major drug dealers when I see them—they usually have weapons, they usually have drugs, and they usually have guns. These folks had nothing. One woman actually had bank records that showed she had done a bank transaction in Oklahoma at the time that she supposedly was selling drugs to an undercover officer in Tulia, Texas. In this case, because of the media spotlight and the work of the NAACP Legal Defense Fund, most of these folks were released from prison. One fellow had actually been sentenced to up to 300 years.

But most of the people who are in prison and who are innocent we never hear about, and that's a topic that really deserves a great deal more attention. Another topic that deserves more attention is the thousands upon thousands of mentally ill people who are in prison. These are people who, in most cases, need some kind of medical treatment. These are people who, in most cases, are not a danger to the public, although in some cases, they might be; but, in any event, they do not belong in prison. Prisons are not mental health facilities. Prisons are places where your mental health deteriorates, not where it improves. So, that's an area where I think that if you had much more of a spotlight, a lot more Americans would be aware of the problems and then maybe—no guarantee—but maybe some small steps could be taken to correct the situation.

The third issue I wanted to mention has to do with employment, or actually the lack of employment. I was out in Chicago not too long ago covering some of the young people who are out of work and out of school. There are 100,000 in Chicago between the ages of sixteen and twenty-four who have dropped out of high school, do not have a high school diploma, and who do not have a job. In New York, there are 200,000 of these young people. And, across the United States, five-and-a-half million.

If you have five-and-a-half million people who are out of school, out of work, and in my view, all but out of hope, you've got a problem. And it is a problem. Not just for them, it's a problem for all of us; it's a problem for the United States of America. So, I think that a lot of the problems that are connected to prison could begin to be alleviated if we looked away from the prison and looked at the conditions in which our young people are coming up. If you look at some of the terrible schools, if you look at the employment situation, and at some point, we have to say, I think, as a society, "enough."

More voices need to be raised; more attention needs to be paid. In my view, you know, you need to raise a little heck. There was a time, I remember, way back in the sixties, when people used to march, when people used to raise their voices, when people used to say, "We will not tolerate these situations anymore." That's where I think we need to get now.

THE CASE OF JONATHAN MAGBIE

by Colbert I. King

Colbert I. King, columnist for the Washington Post, *follows Herbert's broader discussion of innocent populations who are made casualties of the war on drugs, with a discussion of a personal case. Jonathan Magbie, a twenty-seven-year-old African-American quadriplegic, was sentenced to ten days in prison for marijuana possession and died while incarcerated because of failures at every level in the Washington, D.C. criminal justice system. King directly raises the issues of racial profiling and stereotypes in examining the case. What his investigation led him to conclude is an unacceptable failure of any entity to bear even a modicum of accountability in Mr. Magbie's death. King asserts, as does Herbert, that the mainstream press must commit more of its resources to reporting these institutional collapses if they are to be effectively addressed.*

I'm not going to throw a lot of numbers at you. I'm only going to give you one number. I'm going to talk about an African-American young man, named Jonathan Magbie. I wrote six consecutive columns about him. Jonathan Magbie was twenty-seven years old. When he was four, he was involved in an automobile accident that left him as a quadriplegic. He was unable to take care of himself, even to scratch the top of his head. On September 20, 2004, Jonathan Magbie appeared in court, before D.C. Superior Court Judge Judith Retchin, and pleaded guilty to simple possession of marijuana. The government said it had no objection to giving Mr. Magbie probation. The probation officer recommended probation. Judge Retchin sentenced Jonathan Magbie to ten days in the D.C. jail for the possession of marijuana. He arrived at the jail in the afternoon and was processed. About nine o'clock that night, he started to experience respiratory problems. He was taken to Greater Southeast Community Hospital, the hospital that treats D.C. inmates. He was treated, released the next day, and sent back to the jail annex, called the Correctional Treatment Facility.

A doctor at that facility was so disturbed by Jonathan's condition that he called the judge—called her chambers and said, "Because of his condition, he does not belong in this jail." I might mention that Magbie had also told the medical attendants on the night he was incarcerated that he needed a ventilator. He used a ventilator at night. The jail did not have a ventilator.

He went back to the jail on Tuesday. He was there on Wednesday, without a ventilator. He was there on Thursday. Friday morning, he experienced respiratory problems and was taken to the hospital, where he died on September 24.

Why was a first-time quadriplegic offender sentenced to jail? So, I went back and looked at this question. Why did the judge do it? Well, the judge said in open court of the day of sentencing that she had checked with the jail and the jail said it could accommodate his needs.

I talked to the corrections department. They said, "Nobody called us and asked us that question, because if someone had called us and said we were getting a quadriplegic who was ventilator dependent, we would have told them we cannot accommodate a quadriplegic who is ventilator dependent. We didn't know what his condition was until he showed up on the afternoon of September 20."

And then, because of a tip, I got a copy of a transcript of a July 20 bench hearing, in connection with Mr. Magbie. The bench hearing is where they call the attorneys to the front of the court and out of the hearing of the audience, they have a discussion.

It is on that day, July 20, that the government tells the judge, "Judge, the reason we are going to recommend probation and we're not going to ask for incarceration is because we have checked with the jail and they can't accommodate him. As a matter of fact, when he was arrested, we had to take him to the hospital because he needed to be catheterized. That's something that happens every eight or nine hours in his life."

The judge knew three months before she sentenced him that he couldn't be accommodated. So, I talked to the corrections department. I asked, "Why would you accept an inmate who is ventilator dependent if you knew you did not have a ventilator?"

I was told, "Well, we followed the direction from the hospital where we sent him on the first night. They said to give him oxygen, and that's what we did. We gave him oxygen."

"But he needed a ventilator. Your own doctor said he didn't belong there."

"Ah, but we followed the directions of the hospital."

So, I called the hospital and said, "Did you give the corrections department those instructions?"

"We can't talk about it. It's a privacy matter."

Now, let's go back to his arrest. Jonathan Magbie was, in fact, arrested in an area of the city where there's been some drug activity. Jonathan was also in a Hummer. They cost a lot of money, I guess around $70,000.

So, here's a black youth, with another black youth who's driving this vehicle—a 70,000-dollar vehicle—and he's in an area where there might be some drug transactions. Oh, and they found $1,500 on Mr. Magbie. They took him in. Black man, $1,500, Hummer— drug dealing, huh?

No. No. Mr. Magbie, as a result of his settlement for the accident, received $30,000 a month. He had been invested wisely by his mother. She gave him $10,000 a month for spending money. Jonathan Magbie, a quadriplegic, wanted to belong; so he had some of his friends hang out with him, and some of them had been doing drugs, but not Jonathan Magbie.

A gun was found in the car, but even the judge said, "Well, he can't do anything with a gun." The gun was in the car, which was owned by his brother. They lived in a part of the city where there was a lot of car theft, and they argued that the gun was there for protection. I tend to believe it because—as the prosecution said—they had no reason to do crime. They had lots of money.

But Jonathan's gone. I've checked the whole range of players in this scenario—from the police to the judge, from the corrections department to the hospital to the health department (which is supposed to investigate this)—and in a way, they're all culpable.

To me, this is an example of the problem we have with our criminal justice system—from the kind of profiling that takes place by the police, to judges who operate arrogantly and without regard for the people standing before them, to a corrections department that is never held accountable for what it does or fails to do on behalf of inmates, to a press that fails to report on these activities.

I got a letter from his doctor. This doctor wrote: "The travesty is that today our jails are full of Jonathan Magbies, now acting as society's wastebasket for the homeless, the mentally ill, the illiterate, and in Magbie's case, the totally incapacitated." And that's the problem we have with our system.

NOTES

1. Marc Mauer considers the role of mainstream media in framing crime and incarceration in his chapter titled, "Give the Public What It Wants: Media Images and Crime Policy," in *Race to Incarcerate* (New York: The New Press, 2006), pp. 187–194. We would also note, as many analysts have, that color-blind policies have mitigated the social impact of the glaring racial disproportion of incarcerated populations (e.g., though blacks and Latinos comprise approximately 25 percent of the U.S. population, they account for approximately 60 percent of the nation's prisoners).

2. Mauer notes: "More than half the prisons in [the United States] today have been constructed in the last twenty years"(*Race to Incarcerate*, p. 10).

3. Mauer in his chapter titled, "Crime as Politics," in *Race to Incarcerate*, pp. 55–91. It is important to note here, as well, the consequences of the war on drugs as they relate to social constructions of race, specifically stereotypes of black and Latino male identity as inherently "criminal" (*Race to Incarcerate*, pp. 5–15). For an overview of these criminal stereotypes via U.S. popular culture, see Donald Bogle's classic text, *Toms, Coons, Mulattoes, Mammies, and Bucks* (New York: Continuum, 2002); and Charles Ramirez-Berg's *Latino Images in Film: Stereotypes, Subversion, and Resistance* (Austin: University of Texas Press, 2002).

4. Mauer, *Race to Incarcerate*, pp. 12–15.

5. Data obtained from the Sentencing Project (Bureau of Justice statistics). See www.sentencingproject.org.

6. "Report: More women, black men in prison," Associated Press, November 8, 2004. www.msnbc.msn.com/id/6429697/ns/us_news-crime_and_courts/t/report-more-women-black-men-prison/

7. "Facts About the Prison System in the United States," October 4, 2007 at Webb.senate.gov/pdf/prisonfactsheet4.html.

8. See David Eggert, "Michigan is 1 of 4 states to spend more on prison than college," Associated Press, February 28, 2008. www.mlive.com/news/index.ssf/2008/02/michigan_is_1_of_4_states_to_s.html

9. Mauer, *Race to Incarcerate*, pp. 17–18.

10. See Eric Schlosser, "The Prison Industrial Complex," in the *Atlantic Monthly* (December 1998) at www.theatlantic.com/issues/98dec/prisons.htm.

11. Professor Davis's work is widely available on Critical Resistance's website at www.criticalresistance.org.

12. See "Not So Common Language" on Critical Resistance's website.

13. See Lawrence Bobo, James R. Kluegel, and Ryan Smith, "Laissez-Faire Racism: The Crystallization of a Kinder, Gentler, Anti-black Ideology," in *Racial Attitudes in the 1990s: Continuity and Change* (Westport, Conn.: Praeger, 1997), pp. 15–45.

14. 2004 statistics. In January 2011, Detroit public school officials suggested that half the entire system would be closed within two years and class sizes increased to sixty-two students per class (Jennifer Chambers, "Without aid, DPS may close half of its schools," *Detroit News*, January 12, 2011).

15. Mauer, *Race to Incarcerate*, p. 6.

16. Mauer, *Race to Incarcerate*, p. 13.

17. This essay is taken from a speech Mr. Herbert delivered in fall 2004. Dates and events mentioned relate to that time frame.

18. Gabriel London, "DeFriest: Mental Illness Behind Bars," the *Huffington Post*, October 31, 2008. See www.huffingtonpost.com/gabriel-london/defriest-mental-illness-b_b_139696.html.

4

SEGREGATION
and the Urban Crisis

Despite the increasing number of non-white populations in the United States and the important transformation of numerous formerly racially isolated Northern and Southern cities and regions into more diverse areas, racial segregation—particularly in terms of residential housing and education—in our view and that of leading scholars,[1] remains the fundamental cause sustaining urban crisis conditions in America. This is because racial segregation, however relevant to other factors here identified[2] in perpetuating urban inequalities, is directly linked to the production of concentrated poverty,[3] which historically and to the present day has severely limited the abilities of urban black and now subsequent Latino populations to develop economic resources that are essential to effective educational, employment, and related community service institutions. Douglas S. Massey and Nancy A. Denton have focused[4] extensively on the effects of racial segregation in producing urban underclass populations and argue that since the passage of the 1968 Fair Housing Act (which prohibited racial discrimination in housing), residential segregation has ceased to be recognized as an enduring consequence of pervasive discriminatory practices that operated in the United States for most of the twentieth century[5] but is instead now broadly seen as a social phenomenon determined by personal choice and race-neutral economic and civic factors.[6]

This view of segregation, according to Massey and Denton, marks a significant shift from sociological analyses of urban inequalities as early as the mid-1940s and 1950s,[7] as well as civic discourse of the 1960s, including the historic Kerner Commission Report,[8] which emphasized the structural role of racial segregation in fomenting impoverished urban areas. Again, Massey and Denton identify the advent of the Fair Housing Act as a key turning point that reshaped critical and social views of segregation. We would also importantly note that such views of segregation can also be directly related to the emergence of color-blind social and political discourse, specifically as identified by Bonilla-Silva's color-blind frames of "naturalization" and "minimization of racism" (see Chapter 2), which consider segregation as a natural phenomenon or insubstantial structural outcome of U.S. racial politics. We emphasize this relation between civic housing policies and color-blind ideology in order to understand how, as in the case of practices of mass incarceration, residential segregation significantly continues to the present day yet remains a minimal national concern.

Massey and Denton's analysis of segregation in the United States primarily considers black and white populations and has been advanced in more recent critical studies to include Latino and Asian communities, in terms of the multiracial dynamics of residential segregation. As noted, Camille Zubrinsky Charles (see Chapter 1) has identified a racial hierarchy at work that influences neighborhood compositions, one that privileges white identity above all other racial groups (black, Latino, and Asian), while valuing black populations as the least desirable with which to live.[9] Zubrinski Charles's analysis also indicates that among the four racial groups, whites prefer to live in same-race communities at higher rates than nonwhites and are the least willing to integrate among black, Latino, and Asian populations.[10]

This hierarchy of racial tolerance obviously contradicts fundamental tenets of color-blind ideology that regard segregation as a consequence of nondiscriminatory personal choices and/or race-neutral structural forces. Our following contributors provide insight into various arenas in which segregation continues to operate along highly racialized terms that, again, are foundational to urban inequalities.

RACE AND RESIDENTIAL
SEGREGATION IN DETROIT[11]

by john powell and John Telford

powell and Telford offer a powerful commentary on how Detroit's unprecedented racial transformation from a major U.S. city, with a moderate white majority population in the 1970s, to a highly segregated and substantial black majority population in the 1990s[12] is directly linked to the production of concentrated poverty and, indeed, reflective of patterns of racial dynamics in housing and urban areas nationwide. Two key points of their analysis concern the determinative role of white discrimination in influencing the racial composition of residential areas and the recognition that segregation has marginalized the capacity of the city as an entity within broader state electoral politics. Powell and Telford also consider a number of economic and civic strategies by which urban areas can attempt to counteract the deleterious effects of racial segregation.

Many of the most persistent problems of metro Detroit will go unaddressed—and uncorrected—unless we address the issue of racial segregation. Residential segregation is closely tied to economic segregation and the phenomenon known as "concentrated poverty"—when more than 40 percent of the people in a given Census tract are living on incomes below the poverty standard.

In Detroit, the number of impoverished residents rose from 55,913 in 1970 to 418,947 in 1990, and 79.5 percent of them are black. Most of them live in concentrated poverty—neighborhoods that are, in effect, isolated from opportunity. Outside Detroit, this picture is not much improved, as six other major cities within Michigan, including Flint, Grand Rapids, and Jackson, all suffer from significant levels of segregation.

Such conditions engender teenage childbearing and truancy, welfare dependency, the proliferation of AIDS, prostitution, violence, drug abuse, infant mortality, inferior schools and housing, higher in-

surance rates, and price-gouging and profiteering by those who ex-
ploit the people trapped in this economic quarantine. And although
blacks hold the political reins in their segregated neighborhoods,
they are increasingly isolated from state electoral politics, which are
under the control of the white-dominated suburbs.

While many middle-class blacks have migrated to the suburbs, they
continue to face discrimination and isolation. Suburbs such as South-
field, Oak Park, Romulus, and Mt. Clemens have experienced a large
influx of middle-class blacks. But like Detroit before them, they, too,
are undergoing "white flight" and fighting not to succumb to replica-
tion of inner-city conditions, which have become even more exacerbated by the collapse of the U.S. auto industry and global financial
markets. While a majority of whites accept open housing in principle,
they don't support it in practice—and according to numerous recent
demographic studies, white populations are least likely to integrate
with blacks as compared to all other racial groups.

Using data from a 1977 study by the U.S. Department of Housing and Urban Development, George Galster, of Wayne State University, found that white discrimination sets the pattern of racial
residential change. His findings, which have been subsequently
supported by more recent analyses, confirm that skin color is the
organizing determinant of urban housing markets. Race dominates
all other factors that affect where and with whom Americans live.
Galster also found that discrimination not only leads to segregation,
but segregation lowers its victims' economic status.

Residential segregation deprives its victims of access to benefits
that are distributed via housing markets. It is also crucial to understanding how this pattern of impoverishment devastated Detroit.
Black renters and buyers had less money than white residents to
start with, and their efforts to keep up their neighborhoods were
hindered by discrimination by banks and insurance companies. A
growing number of home owners and landlords became afraid to
invest in property maintenance or improvement, leaving their holdings to deteriorate.

Today, white residents move even farther away from Detroit into
new subdivisions built on former farmland—a phenomenon that can

be seen in housing patterns throughout the nation. Small businesses depart to seek more affluent customers. In the city, many neighborhoods are defined by boarded-up, burned-out buildings and vacant lots covered with debris.

This process of robbing resources from the urban core, leaving concentrated poverty behind and pushing the region's edges ever outward could not have occurred without substantial public and private subsidies. Nor can this process be changed without a significant shift in public and private policies and practices.

The political and religious leaders of the Detroit area need to petition HUD to allocate additional funds to fair-housing organizations so they can investigate and prosecute housing discrimination complaints. HUD must also be pressured to establish permanent testing teams of black and white home-seekers to catch real estate agents who discriminate. But it is not enough just to remove the barriers. Our housing pattern, while it was generated by the federal and state governments, now has a life of its own. Throughout our tri-county area, there has to be an affirmative effort to create access for minorities to housing that is close to jobs and other opportunities.

In addition, federal officials should routinely scrutinize banks' lending data to spot suspiciously high rejection rates. To make suits more affordable and speed up judgment, housing discrimination cases should be heard by local judges, with cases going to federal courts only upon appeals. Hate crimes against blacks who integrate and against whites who support them should be prosecuted at the federal level as civil-rights violations. Tax incentives to reintegrate inner-city Detroit and other urban centers should be offered to businesses, residential developers, landlords, and individual home buyers.

Unless we finally tackle the tough task of desegregating Detroit and segregated areas throughout the United States, the toxic effects of residential segregation will continue to poison the aspirations of us all.

HEALTH CARE AS
A CIVIL RIGHTS ISSUE

by Alvin F. Poussaint, MD

One of the most damaging consequences of residential segregation concerns the access of marginalized urban communities to even adequate health care systems and related medical resources on every level (diagnostics, prevention, mental health, etc.), the lack of which has resulted in unconscionable disparities in the overall health conditions of black, white, and Latino populations. Dr. Alvin Poussaint offers a startling commentary of how historically segregated hospitals that operated in the United States, even into the 1960s, provided significantly inferior health care services to African Americans than those facilities that exclusively served white populations and the influence of these practices on contemporary racial health care inequalities. Poussaint makes a crucial assertion, especially in the context of the Obama administration's efforts to achieve health coverage for all Americans, that health care itself has to be defined as a civil rights issue and not merely an issue of economics. Poussaint also importantly addresses conditions of mental health in underclass black communities, linking high rates of suicide and homicide to structural failures in health care and education that we argue are minimized via color-blind discourse and supplanted by stereotypical views of black culture as prone to aggressive and violent behavior.[13]

I am trained as a psychiatrist and a physician. Given my background, I was puzzled during the civil rights movement that health care did not appear as high on the agenda as I would have hoped. Civil rights organizations had the desegregation of schools high on their agendas; they had the integration of public accommodations high on their agendas. But where were health and mental health? When I arrived in Jackson, Mississippi, in June 1965, to work with the civil rights movement, nearly all hospitals in Mississippi were still segregated. Our group—the Medical Committee for Human Rights—made it their top priority to desegregate the heath system.

Health and mental health required urgent attention because segregated health care was a life and death issue for blacks when they received inferior medical care. A message was sent to black people every time they sought health care that their lives were literally not worth as much as white lives. Hospitals and health centers serving black populations shared bad equipment, worn instruments, and torn blankets. Black people actually died in the South because of a lack of—or denial of—health care. Women were turned away from hospitals while they were in labor. When a black person entered an emergency room in a so-called white hospital, with acute symptoms, he or she could be refused treatment. Segregated medicine was a reflection of underlying genocidal attitudes that existed as part of the Southern racist system.

I give this background because at the core of many issues facing us today and what the civil rights struggle has been all about is making a black life count as much as a white life. Now our awareness has expanded to include other minority groups, such as Latinos, Native Americans, and Asians. The fact is that the institutions in our country—educational, criminal justice, and health care—often reflect the reality that a "colored" life is not worth as much as a white life. This ugly truth is apparent when we examine the inequities blacks continue to struggle with today.

The racial disparities in this country's health care systems have been well documented—not just historical disparities, but contemporary ones as well. At birth, the average life expectancy for African Americans is 71.8 years, compared to 77.4 years for whites. African Americans are 30 percent more likely to die of heart disease than whites and are more than twice as likely to die of diabetic complications than whites. In 2000, 47 percent of all cases of HIV/AIDS reported in the United States were among African Americans. Infant mortality rates are more than twice as high for blacks as for whites. The roots of the disparities we experience today lie in the legacies of slavery and our segregated past.

Our history in this country is one of being treated separately and unequally. Our lives have been devalued, and we have been taught to think of our black blood as a taint—something that makes us inferior to whites. To maintain the "peculiar institution" of slavery, it was psychologically necessary for whites to view black Africans as an inferior species. We were never quite human. Slavery left a legacy of indoctrination of psychological inferiority in African-American minds that we still struggle with today.

It is difficult to separate mental health from physical health. If you have diabetes, it is affecting your mental health, not just your body. If you have a stroke, it influences your mental health. If you have a heart disease or HIV/AIDS, it is affecting your mental health. And those groups, not surprisingly, are at higher risk for committing suicide.

In fact, the most dramatic mental health problem in the African-American population is the increase in the suicide rate, particularly among young men. Over the past two decades, the rate of suicide among young black men has more than doubled. While the feminist movement has worked hard to devote programs to women who have traditionally been left out of the men's world, our society must begin to focus on our minority men. If we do not begin to invest more in our black boys and young black men, our society is going to be in deep trouble. The negative statistics regarding young black males are extremely disturbing:

- Homicide is the number one cause of death for black men ages fifteen to thirty-four.
- Only 25 percent of black men currently go to college.
- In 2000, more black men were in jail (791,000) than in college (603,032).

It is no wonder that many of our young black men are discouraged.

Such despair can lead to violence. People commit suicide when they are depressed and feeling hopeless; they believe they have nothing to live for. Some of those same emotional ingredients lead to high homicide rates. If people feel hopeless, they devalue their own lives. If people believe nothing matters for the future—for example, they have no hope of going to college or getting a good job—they will be more likely to kill someone when they are angry or frustrated. And if young men devalue themselves because of their race, they may more readily kill people who look like them.

Witnessing the rising rates of suicide and homicide, many may feel helpless and discouraged. But it is not hopeless; there are ways the black community can alleviate such tragedies. For instance, it is helpful to think of suicide and homicide as existing on a continuum. We see a lot of self-destructive behavior in the black community. If people take self-destructive habits to their logical conclusion, they lead to death. Think of it as slow suicide. Many of these people are desperate, depressed, and/or suffering from mental illness. Under such conditions, people often try to self-medicate with alcohol, drugs, and risky behavior. They may not be actively suicidal, but they don't value living very much. Homicide is similar. One can think of the continuum from minor acts of violence all the way to actual homicide. In both situations, mental health issues need to be addressed.

We need to eliminate the stigma surrounding mental illness. If we refuse to acknowledge mental illness, it will continue to kill us. If a person has a heart attack, we don't tell him to keep a stiff upper lip. We take him to the emergency room. If a person is so full of despair that she is acting like she has a death wish, she needs to get help just as urgently. We also need to understand that health problems such as hypertension, stroke, diabetes, obesity, and heart disease all interconnect with our mental health. If we feel empty inside and eat so much "comfort" food that we become extremely overweight and develop diabetes, that's a mental health problem, as well as a physical problem. You cannot treat only one side of the equation and expect to be effective. We must be holistic in our approach. It is extremely important for the black community to have quality mental health care available to everyone who needs it.

Mental illness is in part a public health problem; using that perspective, we should try to prevent emotional problems before they occur. Many risk factors have to be controlled, but our most focused efforts must be directed at raising strong children. Children raised in households where there is good parenting will have a better chance of growing up to be healthy adults. We live in a society where we have to get a license to drive an automobile and a person has to go to medical school to become a doctor, but an individual is not required to have any training to become a parent. Good parenting is so important that I recommend all public schools provide parenting education for adolescents. At a minimum, parenting education would include required courses in child development, nonviolent discipline, and child care. Knowledge makes a world of difference.

The biggest job any of us have is to raise our children. As a clinician, I have often seen bad things happen not because parents are bad people but because they do not know what children require or what normal behavior is for a young child. For example, a young mother beats her infant because she believes the baby is being "bad" by crying. This mother doesn't understand that a baby is too young to be deliberately bad. Another handicap in some black families is linked to a cultural issue that lingers from slave days; this is the tendency for black parents to beat their children to make them overly obedient. In slave times, an outspoken young black man was likely to become a dead one. While black boys are still at risk in a racist society, it is not appropriate to beat them into passivity. It doesn't work anyway and often backfires. Children who are treated with physical violence are more likely to become enraged and depressed young people, who are more likely to commit suicide and homicide. The vast majority of our incarcerated men and women have been victims of child abuse and neglect.

Good parenting skills are very important to the mental health of the black community because the better care children receive, particularly early in life, the more resilient those children will be in withstanding the hardships they may face in society at large. A resilient child can find a way to succeed and overcome adversity, even under difficult circumstances.

Working together—increasing awareness of mental health problems, making sure that young people can get help when they need it, and supporting parents in their efforts to raise their children—we can lead our youngsters into a better tomorrow.

A CALL FOR
MULTICULTURAL DIALOGUES

by James J. Zogby

Zogby's commentary emphasizes the need for civic and related pub-
lic institutions and the respective communities they serve to develop
and engage in educational programs and multicultural dialogues
that respond directly to the unprecedented demographic change of
the United States into a majority multiracial society. As an example
of this need, Zogby considers the contentious historical and con-
temporary social reactions to the large influx of Arab populations
over the last several decades, and particularly in the aftermath of
9/11, in Dearborn, Michigan, and its neighboring counties, which
currently have the highest concentration of Arab populations in
any area of the world outside of the Middle East.[14] The stereo-
typical views of Arab-American communities that Zogby identifies
are important to consider in the context of race relations between
Detroit and Dearborn in the 1970s (as Michael Omi referenced in
Chapter 2), wherein Dearborn mayor Orville Hubbard advocated
white racial segregation from Detroit's black populations, and in
understanding contemporary residential housing choices as they
involve Arab, Islamic, and multiracial communities.

It was just some seventeen years ago that one of the hot issues in
the Dearborn, Michigan, mayoral race, as it was framed by one of
the candidates, was what to do about what he termed the "Arab
problem." He defined the problem in a mailing he sent to every
household in the city, in which he noted there had been an influx
of Arab immigrants into Dearborn, who were bringing their "foreign
language" and "foreign ways." This, the candidate noted, threatens
"our darn good way of life." More than a decade later, I was in Dearborn at the invitation of a group of Yemeni parents concerned with
the treatment being received by their children in the public schools.
It was Ramadan, the month in which Muslims fast. Instead of being
allowed to go to study hall, the Muslim children were forced to sit

in the cafeteria while the other children ate. They were threatened, they were taunted, food was thrown at them. One of the young Yemeni children—a smart, strong girl about thirteen—organized her classmates and went to see the principal. She told him of their concerns and concluded with a proposal. "The problem," she said, "is that the other children don't know us—our culture. Can we help them know us better?" His response was striking. "Our job," he said, "is not to help you teach us your culture. It's for us to teach you our culture." We often speak of the richness of America's diversity, but we celebrate it only rhetorically. We have been lax about mining this diversity, and so it sits in the ground—an untapped resource. As a result, it also, at times, becomes a source of great tension. In America today, we have more than a crisis in black and white; we have a multicultural crisis of all the shades in between.

The fact is we need a conversation about race in which everyone is included, because when Arabs and Asians and other groups are left out of the conversation, it only leads to increased discrimination and segregation. The danger we face today is that we're all here in southern Michigan but we all live in ghettos. There's a black ghetto and a Polish ghetto and Arab ghettos, but they're all ghettos. Segregation and discrimination are dynamic realities. They create their own agendas, and they spread and grow like disease. We live adjacent to each other. We work together, but we don't know each other or understand each other. We live in proximity, but living in proximity without understanding can be a dangerous and often volatile mix because under these circumstances, we think we know the other groups, when in fact, all we really know are prejudices about them reinforced by anecdote.

Often what we do is take instances of aberrant behavior and elevate them into general observations and conclusions about the group. That's what I call bad science, as in "Oh, I know them. I was in one of their stores, and you know what they're like" or "I know them. They were in my store, and you know what they're like." You see, if we don't mine and explore the richness of our diversity, if we let it lie in the ground, then we are all like the foolish one in the biblical parable—the one who buried his talents. We don't get rewarded.

The question, therefore, before us is what do we do? Former president Clinton had it half right when he launched the One America national conversation about race. I say half right because talking about it while not doing anything to help change behavior or create interaction and understanding was simply not enough. It was ironic, I noted at the time, that while the nation was talking about race, if you went into the White House cafeteria, whites were sitting with whites and blacks were sitting with blacks, repeating a pattern of behavior that we see on our college campuses, in our high school cafeterias, and in our neighborhoods.

We were engineered into this situation of social segregation. We can socially engineer our way out. We can propose programs that bring us together, that break down barriers and create interaction. One such program is called Orientation to Graduation. It is a social engineering program that we take to high schools and colleges, where for one day, children are positioned to eat together in the cafeteria and we can have a class in which children tell their stories about their cultures and histories and learn from each other.

I know the story of Detroit, but I come from Washington, D.C. In Washington, our racial divide is real. It's physical. It's Rock Creek Park. One side of the city's white and the other side of the city is black. And do you know what? Many people in northwest D.C. have never been to northeast D.C. in their entire lives and never been to Anacostia, because you just don't go there. I prepared a study for Washington, called Cross Worship. In it, I proposed that on one Sunday or one Friday, people on one side of town adopt a church, synagogue, or mosque on the other and cross-worship or eat with one another—something we almost never do in our homes. I proposed that our city governments create ward-by-ward commissions that bring together businessmen, religious leaders, and parents not only to solve problems but to tell stories and learn from each other about our cultures and histories.

In this city, some wonderful efforts are already under way. For example, there's the Concert of Colors. My own community has the Arab festival. The Arab Chamber of Commerce and the Arab Community Center for Economic Social Services (ACCESS) have also sponsored an Arab and American summit. They're trying to mine the resource, but as the horrors of 9/11 and the backlash that followed taught us, much remains to be done to respond to the plea of my little Yemeni friend. Those who go to the cultural festivals and who visit ACCESS or participate in community discussions don't need an answer. The challenge before us is to engage in a programmatic way for those who do need more understanding, for those who do need to hear the stories and who need to be challenged to break out of their own segregated ghettos.

AMERICAN EDUCATION: STILL SEPARATE, STILL UNEQUAL[15]

by Arthur Levine

Levine's essay provides a sobering overview of the nation's efforts to achieve integration in public education in the aftermath of the historic 1954 Supreme Court decision, Brown v. Board of Education, *which outlawed legal segregation in public schooling. His conclusion, which has been echoed by leading educators,[16] is that more than half a century following the Brown ruling the U.S. public school system remains potently segregated, with millions of lower-income black and Latino students marginalized in schools with vastly inadequate educational resources, standing in stark contrast to predominantly white and affluent school districts that effectively prepare students for successful college and university careers. The decisive failure of Brown (which scholars such as Gary Orfield and Derrick Bell[17] have linked to subsequent court decisions and/or policy actions that allowed states to avoid implementing viable integration programs, particularly under the Reagan administration[18] in the 1980s) is rendered even more problematic by recent Supreme Court rulings against affirmative action in higher education and the June 2007 ruling against voluntary integration programs in Seattle, Washington and Louisville, Kentucky school districts.[19] We will discuss this latter ruling in more detail in our next chapter ("Education and the Urban Crisis") but will argue, as with the persistent phenomenon of racial segregation in residential housing, that color-blind discourse has reframed social views of race to the extent that segregation in public schools is largely seen as a matter of choice and not structural consequence. Levine exposes this fallacy by locating the nation's educational crisis in the context of the development of a new civil rights movement itself, one that he argues will be necessary if we are to overcome the inherent racial inequalities of public education that have operated throughout the entire history of the United States.*

When [former] President Bush decided to intervene on behalf of plaintiffs in a pair of lawsuits against the University of Michigan, he reignited a contentious national debate about affirmative action. But the discussion will be incomplete unless it also addresses the most serious civil rights issue in America today: inequality of education.

In a world of equal opportunity and funding for elementary and high school education, affirmative action would wither in importance in higher education. But in America today, vast numbers of children don't have access to the kind of elementary school and high school educations that prepare them for college admissions.

Twenty years ago, reformers embarked on a campaign to improve the nation's schools. At that time, suburban schools were strong, and urban and rural schools were poor. Today, suburban schools are even stronger; urban and rural schools remain poor. In two decades, with Houston perhaps a hotly debated exception, the nation has failed to turn even one urban school district around.

So what has been accomplished? The school reform movement gave the middle class more choices. There are now charter and magnet schools and public schools with selective admissions policies. Most cities now have a smattering of quite strong elementary schools, and with their good consumer skills, middle-class parents have done well in identifying and getting their children into them. There are also more lower-cost private schools—usually Catholic or otherwise religiously affiliated. And with suburban schools stronger than ever, middle-class families can move if no urban options are appealing.

The result is that most students left in failing inner-city public schools now come from low-income and minority families. They attend schools funded at lower rates, which means their teachers are paid lower salaries than suburban teachers. They are far more likely to have teachers who lack certification, and their curriculum materials are likely to be inadequate in number and in poorer condition than at suburban schools. Their facilities are in far poorer shape.

A huge gap in achievement exists between minority and majority students and between students attending urban and suburban schools. We have two school systems: one for affluent children, another for the poor. We have a set of schools largely for black and Latino students and another, far better, largely for whites. Once again, we have created, not by design but by happenstance, a system of separate and unequal education.

We are unlikely to do much about it. The economy is weak and cuts will certainly be made in domestic programs. Tax cuts seem more popular than investments in urban schools and low-income children, anyway. But for the sake of our future, the country needs to be shaken from its complacency. Providing a quality education for every child needs to be seen as a national obligation, not a future hope or an impractical utopian ideal.

If we are to bring about this change, what will be necessary is a civil rights movement in which the goal is to establish a quality education as the right of every child. There will need to be litigation aimed at getting the courts to require not equal funding for urban and suburban schools but adequate funding for urban and rural schools. Because working conditions will always be more difficult in urban schools, they will need additional funds to pay higher salaries in order to compete successfully for the best teachers in the country.

We will need campaigns in every state for an educational bill of rights for children, guaranteeing each child the essentials of a quality education—a well-prepared teacher, up-to-date curriculum materials, a safe physical plant, and a school that has demonstrated it can prepare students to perform at grade level. Students at schools failing to meet these criteria should be allowed to transfer, at state expense, to schools that do.

To bring these issues to the fore will undoubtedly also require voter-registration and get-out-the-vote campaigns, as inner-city residents are less likely than those in the suburbs to go to the polls. Parents in poor communities with failing schools should stand firm in voting as a bloc for whichever political party offers the strongest platform for improving urban education. They should make clear that if promises are not kept, even more voters will show up the next time to turn them out. This could be a very potent force. It would also be valuable to organize local communities to take to the streets, peacefully, to demand better schools.

Hand in hand with voting and demonstrations needs to come parent education—teaching parents how to use consumer skills in choosing schools, how to advocate for their children, ask questions about education, and how to understand their educational rights and options.

Finally, charter schools need to be used as a weapon against failing schools. Most states now have laws allowing for the creation of new public schools with greater flexibility. Parents whose children are consigned to poor schools need to be able to establish such schools to move recalcitrant school bureaucracies.

Affirmative action comes too late for the many low-income and minority children who drop out of failing schools before completing high school. They need opportunities that begin in kindergarten— the kind affluent children already have.

NOTES

1. Douglas S. Massey and Nancy A. Denton make a forceful argument in *American Apartheid: Segregation and the Making of the Underclass* (Cambridge, Mass.: Harvard University Press, 1993), asserting that the United States has produced a "culture of segregation" (p. 8) that has acutely affected black populations more than any other racial group, a phenomenon they subsequently define as "hypersegregation" (pp. 74–82). Gary Orfield's noted work on segregation can be found at the Civil Rights Project/ Proyecto Derechos Civiles website at www.civilrightsproject.ucla.edu. Also, see Thomas Sugrue's brief review of scholarship in *The Origins of the Urban Crisis: Race and Inequality in Postwar Detroit* (Princeton, N.J.: Princeton University Press, 1996), p. 282, note 5.

2. For example, see Reynolds Farley, Sheldon Danziger, and Harry J. Holzer, *Detroit Divided* (New York: Russell Sage Foundation, 2002), pp. 6–13 and Thomas J. Sugrue, *The Origins of the Urban Crisis: Race and Inequality in Postwar Detroit* (Princeton, N.J.: Princeton University Press, 1986). Massey and Denton note, however, that urban underclass scholarship in the 1970s and 1980s mitigated the role of segregation in producing urban crisis conditions (*American Apartheid*, pp. 1–16), a critical view which they reject entirely and we would argue has tended to support color-blind paradigms of racial inequality.

3. powell and Telford define "concentrated poverty" as a condition in which "40 percent of the people in a given census tract are living on incomes below the poverty standard."

4. Massey and Denton, *American Apartheid*, pp. 83–114.

5. "Following the passage of the Fair Housing Act in 1968, the problem of housing discrimination was declarcd solved, and residential segregation dropped off the national agenda" (Massey and Denton, *American Apartheid*, p. 4.).

6. See Bonilla-Silva's discussion of the color-blind frame of "Abstract Liberalism," in *Racism Without Racists: Color-Blind Racism and the Persistence of Racial Inequality in the United States* (New York: Rowman & Littlefield, 2006), pp. 30–36. Also, see Douglas S. Massey and Mary J. Fischer, "Where We Live, in Black and White," in the *Nation* 267(20) (December 1998), p. 25. Massey and Fischer's commentary is important here for its analysis of declining rates of segregation in U.S. urban areas, which the authors argue are misleading and have had little effect on overall racial segregation.

7. Massey and Denton, *American Apartheid*, pp. 3–4. Here we refer to Massey and Denton's analysis of Myrdal's (*An American Dilemma: The Negro Problem and Modern Democracy*) and Clark's (*Dark Ghetto: Dilemmas of Social Power*) works.

8. See, for example, "King and Kerner: An Unfinished Agenda," by Edward W. Brooke, one of the original authors of the 1968 Kerner Commission Report, in the *Washington Post*, April 3, 2008, A-17.

9. See Camille Zubrinsky Charles, "Can We Live Together?: Racial Preferences in Neighborhood Outcomes," in *The Geography of Opportunity: Race and Housing Choice in Metropolitan America*, edited by Xavier de Souza Briggs (Washington, D.C.: Brookings Institution Press, 2005), pp. 50–63.

10. Zubrinsky Charles considers several factors at work here in producing this racial hierarchy, including class and ethnocentric explanations, but she argues that for "all racial groups, the effect of racial stereotyping is always stronger and more consistent than that of perceived social class differences or in-group attachment" (*The Geography of Opportunity*, pp. 63–76).

11. A shorter version of this article appeared in the *Detroit Free Press*, on May 5, 1999.

12. See endnote 2 in Preface. We would again point to Detroit's unprecedented racial transformation from a majority white city to a majority black city in the ten-year span from 1970 to 1980 as pivotal here, with an emphasis on the effects of public school desegregation on white popula-

tions in the city, who, we would argue, following the analysis of Zubrinsky Charles and Krysan (see endnote 7 in Chapter 1), were far less likely to participate in school integration than black populations.

13. We would simply point to the glaring racial inequalities in the U.S. prison system, which have been driven by *policy* and not actual *behavior*, as a related analogy here.

14. Source: The Arab American Institute. See www.aaiusa.org/

15. An earlier version of this essay was originally published as an op-ed in the *Los Angeles Times* in 2003.

16. See endnote 2 in Preface. Gary Orfield has published extensively on this subject. See, for example, Gary Orfield and Chungmei Lee, "'Brown at 50': King's Dream or 'Plessy's' Nightmare?" (Cambridge, Mass.: Harvard Civil Rights Project, 2004); and Gary Orfield and Susan E. Eaton, *Dismantling Desegregation: The Quiet Reversal of Brown v. Board of Education* (New York: The New Press, 1996).

17. Orfield and Lee, "'Brown at 50'"; Orfield and Eaton, *Dismantling Desegregation*; and Derrick Bell, *Silent Covenants: Brown v. Board of Education and the Unfulfilled Hopes for Racial Reform* (New York: Oxford University Press, 2004).

18. Orfield and Eaton, *Dismantling Desegregation*; Michael Omi and Howard Winant, *Racial Formation in the United States: From the 1960s to the 1990s* (New York: Routledge, 1994), p. 134; and Andrew J. Polosky and Daniel M Cook, "Political Time Reconsidered: Unbuilding and Rebuilding the State Under the Reagan Administration," *American Politics Research* 33(4), 2005, pp. 577–605.

19. See extensive discussions of this case (*Parents Involved in Community Schools v. Seattle School District No. 1*) via the Kirwan Institute for the Study of Race and Ethnicity (see endnote 10 in Chapter 2) and the Civil Rights Project/Proyecto Derechos Civiles (see endnote 1 in this chapter).

5

EDUCATION
and the Urban Crisis

A s discussed in the previous chapter, the U.S. public school system continues to function in segregated and unequal terms that both severely limit the educational outcomes of primarily black and Latino urban underclass populations and perpetuate a broad spectrum of structural urban crisis conditions, which also influence social views of racial identity as well (e.g., as noted, historical and contemporary ideas that black and Latino cultures are pathological and that such pathology accounts for disparities in educational and economic achievement in contrast to white and "model minority" populations).[1]

While a detailed discussion of the history, operations, and continuing effects of these "two separate school systems" (see Levine in Chapter 4) that structure U.S. public education has been well documented,[2] our focus concerns the June 2007 Supreme Court decision against voluntary integration programs in the Seattle, Washington and Louisville, Kentucky public school districts (*Parents Involved in Community Schools v. Seattle School District No. 1* [*PICS*]),[3] which we feel highlights key issues as they relate to contemporary views of the role of racial integration in public education and the challenges to traditional models of pedagogy in the context of an ever-increasing multiracial society.

Though citing several legal reasons, Chief Justice Roberts's plurality opinion[4] in the *PICS* case is primarily based on the argument that the Seattle and Louisville districts' utilization of race as a factor in achieving integration is merely a form of "racial balancing,"[5] which, via established precedent, is prohibited by the U.S. Constitution. Additionally, the Roberts opinion rejects arguments citing the benefits of integration in public education despite substantive research to the contrary.[6]

In arguing that the plans in *PICS* are merely forms of racial balancing, Roberts asserts that the historical effects of legal segregation in sustaining contemporary racial inequalities in public education cannot be remedied by integration unless the government (or related entity) is responsible for producing such segregation. Absent this, Roberts argues that contemporary segregation in public schools has to be regarded as a consequence of private decisions that have no relevant structural origins.[7] This view, severing segregation from its historical context, is again reflective of key frames of color-blind ideology that regard segregation as a natural result of voluntary actions and, we will argue, has been so influential in eliminating efforts to achieve public school integration during the last three decades that even such widely recognized integration advocates as Charles Ogletree, Jr. and Derrick Bell[8] have withdrawn from the aims of integration and instead focused on improving educational equality and achievement without concern for racial diversity in schools.

While we understand this position given the intractable history of segregation in the United States and what scholars have recently identified as the "re-segregation"[9] of our public schools, we disagree with it in principle. It reflects, in our view, a retreat from discursive strategies of race, which we feel are essential to redress racial inequalities, especially in the advent of the election of Barack Obama. His election to president of the United States represents historically significant racial progress but has also galvanized fallacious color-blind views that racial discrimination no longer exerts any relevant influence in the United States.

As our contributors in this chapter argue, the nation's overall public education system itself needs to be transformed and specifically in race-conscious terms that respond to the multiracial demographics of U.S. populations. It is our firm belief that the United States will never truly achieve democracy unless systemic segregation, as it operates in virtually all aspects of American society, is eliminated. Moreover, if we are to subvert the stereotypes that currently drive racial attitudes and segregation, then reclaiming the language of race from the speciousness of color-blind discourse is paramount.

TOWARD A PARADIGM SHIFT IN OUR CONCEPT OF EDUCATION

by Grace Lee Boggs

Legendary educator and civil rights activist, Grace Lee Boggs gives an incisive critique of the failures of public schools to meaningfully engage students in ways that encourage their intellectual development outside the dictates of long-established "factory model" approaches to education that are no longer applicable in contemporary post-industrial (informational/service) economies. Traditional educational paradigms, according to Boggs, take a "mechanistic" view of students, which privileges the ability to simply memorize and regurgitate information while virtually ignoring community service-learning pedagogical approaches that emphasize the relevance of education to the real-world conditions of students. Boggs's central argument is that when students perceive their actions can produce positive transformations of their actual living and educational environments, they are far more likely to succeed in school and contribute to the development of their communities and society at large. The institutionalization of a service-learning curriculum in public education could also provide a means of unprecedented collaboration among schools proximately located in otherwise highly segregated districts that are, however, mutually engaged in projects from which all could potentially derive social and economic benefits.[10]

More than thirty years ago, after having been heavily involved in the struggle for community control of schools, I made a speech on education in Detroit that has been widely reprinted in journals, including the *Harvard Educational Review*, and also as a pamphlet titled, *Education to Govern*, which went through three printings. In that speech, I warned that in the light of the urban rebellions that

---

Reprinted with permission from Grace Lee Boggs, *The Next American Revolution* (Berkeley, April 2011).

have brought black youth onto the historical stage, we need to go beyond community control and begin grappling with fundamental questions about the purpose of education and how children learn.

The time has come, I said, to go beyond the top-down factory model of education, which was created at the beginning of the century to supply industry with a disciplined work force. In order to transform our children from angry rebels into positive change agents, our schools need to give them a sense of the unique capacity of human beings to shape and create reality in accordance with conscious purposes and plans.

Learning must be related to the daily lives of children. It is not something you can make people do in their heads, with the perspective that, eventually, they will get a good job and make a lot of money, or as the saying goes "get somewhere." Our schools, I said, need to be transformed to provide children with ongoing opportunities to exercise "their resourcefulness to solve the real problems of their communities." Children will be motivated to learn and their cognitive juices will begin to flow because their hearts, heads, and hands are engaged in improving their daily lives and their surroundings.

In the decades that have elapsed since 1969, our schools and communities have deteriorated far beyond anything that I could have imagined. As corporations have exported jobs out of our communities and the information revolution has brought us to the threshold of a post-industrial society, our schools have continued to operate on the factory model. So 35 to 50 percent of inner-city youth drop out, many of them becoming trapped in the drug economy and ending up in prison, because they are no longer willing to sit passively in classrooms for twelve or more years, receiving and regurgitating information, when all around them the need for change and for critical and creative thinking is so obvious.

The factory-model school is based on the profoundly antidemocratic belief that only experts are capable of creating the knowledge that teachers then deliver in the form of information and students give back on tests. Like workers in the factory, children and young people are treated as cogs whose "job" is to ingest basics in order to survive, consume, and produce. Most educators still practice this model, which worked fairly well in the first half of the twentieth century, when this country was pioneering mass production and when most children from working-class families went to school for only a few years. Its limitations didn't become glaring until the 1960s, when we began to move toward a post-industrial society at the same time that young people, through rebellions at both the university and street level, proclaimed their right to be full participants in deciding this country's direction.

Since then our schools have been in continuing crisis because so few educators are able or willing to take the risk of leaving behind the old factory model and creating a new one that meets the human and social need of young people to be creators of knowledge and of social change. Parents have not been much help because their fears for their children's survival have led them to stress staying in school to get a job. So millions of young people, coming of age in a new world where information is everywhere and industrial work is disappearing, experience schooling as boring, a denial of their humanity and a kind of incarceration.

It is not going to be easy to relinquish this "Command and Control" model of schooling. To do so we need the incentive that comes from recognizing how many of our children have already left it behind. We also need a new philosophy in which students are not viewed mechanistically (or from a Newtonian perspective) but as human beings, who like all human beings, regardless of age, ethnicity, gender, or national origin, are capable of self-organization, self-reflection, and creativity. Recent studies of the brain and mind support the need for a paradigm shift in our concept of education.

For example, in *Education on the Edge of Possibility* (Association for Supervision and Curriculum Development, 1991), Renata and Geoffrey Caine explain that today's schools fail because they see brainpower only as memorization instead of building on the multiple and complex powers of the human brain. Among these are the capacity to function on many levels simultaneously, to change in response to others, to keep searching for meaning, to create patterns, to enrich ideas by linking them to emotions and all the senses, to simultaneously perceive and create, to be inhibited by threats (like rewards and punishment), and to be enhanced by challenges and opportunities to make a difference.

Schooling that denies children and young people the right to exercise these capacities produces individuals who are in a constant state of rebellion and are therefore perceived by the adult world as threats to an orderly society.

On the other hand, education that gives children the freedom to exercise their powers creates the kind of socially responsible, visionary, and creative young people whom we urgently need as change agents in the daily lives of our communities.

In his book, *The Hand: How Its Development Shaped the Brain, Languages and Human Culture* (Random House, 1998), Frank R. Wilson, a practicing neurologist, describes how he became fascinated with the role of the hand in the evolution of the human race and the development of the mind because of his experiences (1) as an adult trying to learn how to play the piano and (2) as a doctor working with patients who have difficulty using their hands. After intensive study, Wilson became convinced that one of the major reasons for the crisis in our schools is that we have underestimated the role of the hand. Because our society has made such a sharp separation between the mind and the body and because we are so prejudiced against manual labor, we have created a brain-centered (cephalocentric) educational system based on the illusion that we can educate the mind by itself.

This system doesn't work because it violates the way that learning actually takes place. Biologically the head and the hand evolved together. As Wilson states: "For the brain to work it needs information that can only come from the hand acting on objects or from tactile and kinesthetic perception. . . . There is not, and cannot be . . . anything called intelligence, independent of the behavior of the entire organism, or of its entire and exclusive history of interactions with the world. . . . The attainment of early language milestones in the child always takes place in company with the attainment of very specific motor milestones."

Our schools actually do violence psychologically to children because we fill their minds with information and confine them to classrooms, divorcing them from physical activity and the physical world at a time when they need to know what the world really is about. That is why we urgently need a paradigm shift in our concept of the purposes and practices of education. We need to leave behind the concept of education as a passport to more money and higher status in the future and replace it with a concept of education as an ongoing process that enlists the tremendous energies and creativity of schoolchildren in rebuilding and respiriting our communities and our cities now, in the present.

During Mississippi Freedom Summer in 1964, civil rights activists created Freedom Schools because black schools in the South had been organized to produce subjects, not active citizens. Black children were encouraged to see themselves as part of a social movement. That is the kind of schooling we need today.

Just think of how much safer, healthier, and livelier our communities would become almost overnight if as a natural and normal part of the curriculum from K–12, school children were taking responsibility for maintaining neighborhood streets, planting community gardens, recycling waste, creating healthier school lunches, organizing neighborhood festivals, relating to elders. This is the fastest way to motivate all our children to learn and at the same time turn our communities into lively neighborhoods where crime is going down because hope is going up.

This is not an idle dream. In 1992, recalling how Martin Luther King, Jr., in response to the urban rebellions, had proposed self-transforming and structure-transforming projects for Negro [sic] youth in "our dying cities," we founded Detroit Summer, a multicultural intergenerational program to involve young people in community projects to rebuild, redefine, and respirit Detroit from the ground up.

Every summer, for the last twelve years, teams of middle and high school youth have organized themselves to turn vacant lots into community gardens and parks, paint public murals, rehab houses, engage neighborhood youth in a bike recycling program, and at the same time explore new ideas about economics, transportation, education, and social change. Every year Detroit Summer is attracting more college students preparing to become teachers and looking for new ways to break down the walls between the classroom and the community.

Detroit Summer is creating a fluid model that can be adopted and adapted by all kinds of community groups and schools. Kids Involved in Doing Service (KIDS) is a community-building program that has been developed for public school children in the de-industrialized cities of New England. Students at the Moretown Elementary School in Vermont, for example, researched the feasibility of planting trees along the banks of the Mad River to decrease thermal impact on the river, absorb runoff, and enhance animal habitats.

Middle school students in Bath, Maine, mapped an historical walking tour of downtown Bath for distribution by the chamber of commerce, local restaurants, and information centers. Lewiston Middle School students restored the interior and exterior appearance of their historic building. You can find out more about KIDS at www.kidsconsortium.org.

Ten years ago the Pew Charitable Trust, recognizing the overwhelming desire of young people to act on behalf of the environment and to help their communities through voluntary service, created Earth Force, a program that involves schoolchildren in monitoring water quality and solving other environmental problems in their communities. In Ypsilanti, Michigan, a nonprofit organization calling itself Creative Change Educational Solutions (CCES) provides teachers with training and materials that enable their students to make a connection between the environment, their communities, and the economy.

These materials are aligned with national and state standards and can be easily integrated into economics, civics, language, and/or science classes. Teachers who have been trained by CCES talk about how exciting it is to teach in this way. Test scores rise because the kids see themselves in the hands-on projects. Instead of depending on the teacher to decide the lessons, the kids bring lessons to the classroom based on their own experiences, for example, monitoring air quality, something that means a lot in urban settings, where many students use inhalers. Creative change teaching, the teachers say, incorporates core democratic values because it helps kids see that their food, transportation, and housing choices matter.

If we're serious about democracy, this is the way we have to teach. Students have to be able to see, feel, hear what they're studying and see that it actually makes a difference in their lives. Programs like Detroit Summer, KIDS, Earth Force, and Creative Change Educational Solutions provide children and young people with opportunities to take ownership of problems or issues affecting their school and their town. Thereby, they give meaning to the lives of our children in the present while preparing them to become active citizens in a democratic society. At the same time they foster the culture of hope and change in the community, which is something we all need, whether we live in the inner city or the suburbs.

WRITING AND MULTIRACIAL EDUCATION

by Nell Irvin Painter

Echoing critical ideas of James Zogby (Chapter 4) and Grace Lee Boggs, Nell Irvin Painter comments on the role of writing and the need to develop specialized writing programs in public schools to foster multiracial dialogues that will encourage broader social understanding and collaborations between segregated communities in Detroit and racially polarized regions throughout the nation. Two key points that Painter makes concern the issue of how racial identity influences constructions of American history, which she highlights via the example of Southern narratives of the Civil War as the "Lost Cause,"[11] and the prevailing influence of color-blind discourse on race relations and efforts to respond to continuing racial inequalities. Painter's methodological approach could be easily incorporated into various programs identified by Boggs and applied within early levels of education, where dialogues of race and diversity are often very difficult to engage.

Dr. Curtis L. Ivery has said: "The time has come to move beyond rhetoric, to develop initiatives that will produce structural changes. . . . We must also recognize that these structural interventions will only be temporary unless we affect to change the American consciousness itself, where all people are compelled to engage these issues in order to fulfill the ideals of democracy."

This statement needs to always be kept in mind, for we must advance the goal of changing consciousness, especially white consciousness, and to do that, we need to find new strategies. This particular goal is an instrumental one. It is not epistemological. It is not the same as teaching the facts of American history or getting people to agree on those facts.

Inner-city communities have been isolated, and we are asked to think of means to break through that isolation. We are trying to find ways of bringing people together who have been separated in their own urban black and Latino and suburban white spaces and who see the meaning of American life in different ways. For this audience and its allies, the fact of institutional racism does not constitute any kind of discovery. We've known forever that institutional racism has a long and very deep history in our country.

In his essay, Houston Baker has summed up the historical situation and diagnosed the problems very clearly. But returning to Dr. Ivery's charge, the question remains of how to change the consciousness of all sorts of Americans, allies and non-allies. To do that, we can't simply talk to ourselves and our close allies; we also need to talk to people—white people—who see the world in very different ways, especially as they represent the majority of Americans and exert enormous political influence. If we simply reinforce what we already know, we end up more and more isolated. We will not have broken through to the white people, who do not see the world as we do.

My remedy for changing consciousness and bringing together urbanites and suburbanites is simple: writing to each other about their own lives. Young people of all races and ethnicities should write to each other of their daily experiences and their life's hopes. They need to communicate with each other as individuals, each with his or her own particular experiences, not to persuade others to think the way they do, but to get to know one another as real people. Autobiographical writing can serve two ends, intellectual and political. Before I flesh out my recommendation, let me explain how I came to draw the conclusion that getting to know people can change consciousness and break down isolation.

I draw my remedy from the experience of Southern history. Before the civil rights revolution of the 1950s and 1960s, the majority of Americans accepted naïve ideas about the history of the American South. Those ideas consisted of vaguely misty memories of the Lost Cause and moonlight-and-magnolias—a *Gone with the Wind* Southern history. According to this view, everything was just fine in the 1950s, and the races were adjusted perfectly. Supposedly, Southerners of all races and classes, whether black or white, whether employers or workers, were all like a family. Everything was fine.

Although this was the prevailing notion, it was not the only view of Southern history in existence.

There was another view, and it finally triumphed, as masses of Americans learned how black Southerners were actually mistreated under segregation. The other history, much less known in the 1950s, included slavery and oppression and the sundering of families and trauma and violence and night riding and lynching. Above all, it rejected segregation and white supremacy as right or natural. This version of Southern history appeared on the television news, as white supremacists shed black blood in the most savage ways in order to preserve segregation. African-American writers, such as James Baldwin and Maya Angelou, depicted black life stories with riveting artistry. Martin Luther King Jr. showed how racism narrowed the chances of his own family. Bringing Southern violence to light as something that crippled real people's lives helped defeat it.

In the 1950s and 1960s, remedies to oppression lay in government action that affected people as a group. This is no longer entirely the case. Today is not the 1960s, as you well know. Some of you will remember that the 1960s came after the 1940s and the 1930s. The 1960s were a moment when the union movement was much stronger and also racial segregation was much stronger, so people had a clearer sense of their identities as groups.

Today, group remedies are rather out of political favor. Americans, especially young people, are likely to think of themselves differently. Young white people, especially, think of themselves purely as individuals. Their version of American society can differ radically from that of Americans who are not white. A deeply held sense among many white people is that racism is over. They think "I wasn't here, I didn't do it; I'm innocent. Besides, why can't we just get over this race thing?" White people can see others, notably African Americans, as so different as to be unfathomable, so different as to lack political common interests, so different as to be foreigners.

This sense of foreignness isolates our urban communities.

This is where writing comes in—writing about one's own life to people who do not know it. This is writing as a means of breaking down isolation—two or three young people at a time writing to each other, letting each other know about others across lines of race and ethnicity.

I do not mean that students should share their first writing, for that would not yet be likely to reach into individual consciousness. First attempts would probably reach for easy identification and ready-made formulae: notions quickly picked up from popular culture and short-cut identification. I mean writing that is more thoughtful and personal than first drafts. Writers should keep writing regularly, to reach their humanity and their complex identity as individuals. I know that a lot of teachers will read this, and I know that you probably have seen how those barriers can fall down when young people are working together in a sport or on some kind of project.

Dr. Grace Lee Boggs mentions the positive outcomes of such group projects in Detroit. I believe that writing serves two ends: intellectual and political. Let me elaborate. Most teachers recognize immediately the cognitive work writing does. As we write, we think, and the more we write, the more clearly we think. As a means of encouraging young people to think critically, writing serves a crucial purpose. In addition, writing is the tool Americans need to succeed socially and economically.

Writing can also serve political ends by breaking down the barriers between people in the city and in the suburbs. When people communicate the particulars of their lives, they create empathy and understanding. Breaking down racial barriers is a good thing of itself, but in addition, reducing our urban communities' political isolation holds additional promise. People who know one another as individuals are much less likely to dismiss the problems of people they know. They're more likely to see common interests across lines of city and suburb. Inequities that affect people whose lives they know are more likely to be inequities that will be addressed.

Writing pays off in many, many ways: It fosters critical thought; it gives every author a larger sense of self; it reaches out to others across lines of geography, race, ethnicity, and gender. In present circumstances, writing offers a way to build intellectual bridges conveying human empathy and political cooperation.

POLICE IN SCHOOLS: CAN A LAW ENFORCEMENT ORIENTATION BE RECONCILED WITH AN EDUCATIONAL MISSION?[12]

by Johanna Wald and Lisa Thurau

Wald and Thurau's essay focuses on educational and law enforcement practices in public schools, including zero tolerance policies, and their relation to ever-increasing numbers of young populations who become involved in the U.S. juvenile criminal justice system. As with the adult criminal justice system, non-whites constitute a significantly disproportionate number of young populations who face some form of incarceration, comprising 70 percent of those entering juvenile court in 2002.[13]

Wald and Thurau also importantly note that a "school-to-prison pipeline" has emerged within the U.S. educational system as a result of failed public school policies that emphasize law enforcement above all else as a primary response to a broad range of student behaviors that could be resolved far more constructively without recourse to the criminal justice system. The authors offer several recommendations that states and districts can adopt to improve educational and social outcomes.

OVERVIEW

Today, in public schools across the country—urban, rural, and suburban; elementary, middle, and secondary—police are a familiar sight, in the hallways, outside on the playgrounds, and at building entrances. School resource officers (SROs), as they are commonly called, supervise dances and athletic events, and roam the cafeteria during lunch. Many teach classes and even coach sports teams. The police squad car now often sits alongside the yellow school buses in the parking lot. A generation of children have progressed through school believing police officers to be as daily a part of their adult school community as teachers, principals, and guidance counselors.

Yet, a decade after police have become ubiquitous in public schools, their purpose and effect remain shrouded in mystery. The responsibilities and goals of SROs are often subject to very different interpretations by police and school officials, and poorly understood by students and parents. Surprisingly, little data are available concerning how their presence affects overall school environment; how they interact with teachers, principals, students, or parents; or how they reconcile tensions that crop up when a law enforcement orientation conflicts with an educational mission.

This confusion and ambiguity are partly due to the accelerated rate with which police officers have entered public schools. The numbers have increased from an estimated 9,446 in 1997 to a current presence of approximately 17,000 nationally.[14] This escalation came about through the convergence of several interrelated events, including (1) the availability of federal funds to support police in schools through the Community Oriented Policing Services (COPS) program; (2) high-visibility shootings in schools, which created a wave of fear about violence and harsh new zero tolerance policies in schools; and (3) passage of new laws stiffening penalties against juvenile offenders in every state.

In the process, two camps rapidly formed concerning the role of police in schools. Those in favor argue that a police presence is a necessary and positive step to preventing violence and crime in school. They cite the comfort that students, parents, and school officials take from knowing a police officer is nearby at all times during the day. Those opposed maintain that a constant police presence is in conflict with an educational mission, that the "teachable moment" is being replaced by a law enforcement approach to all student misbehaviors, and that relatively minor school code violations that once would mean a trip to the principal's office are now being criminalized.[15] They point to incidences of children being arrested for "disorderly conduct" for shoving another student in the hallway or "disrupting the peace" for flicking a rubber band during a school assembly. They cite evidence showing that police presence in schools fuels the "school-to-prison pipeline"—a term used to describe the process by which youths, disproportionately poor and of color, are pushed out of school and into the criminal justice system.[16]

This paper summarizes major findings from a series of interviews that the authors conducted in 2008 and 2009 with police chiefs and school resource officers in sixteen school districts in Massachusetts. Our goal was to hear directly from the police themselves about how they viewed their job and responsibilities and how they interacted with students, parents, and school officials. At the end of the paper, we include recommendations for reforms to the school resource officer programs as presently implemented, which we believe will maximize the benefits they provide to schools and communities, while reducing risk of unnecessary criminalization of youths.

MAJOR FINDINGS

1. Contrary to the assumptions of many, there is tremendous variation in approaches to school policing.

At one end of the continuum, some departments espoused an authoritarian/zero tolerance approach, in which surveillance and reports of misconduct, ranging from fistfights to verbal altercations, put youths at risk of arrest—whatever the context. On the other end, one SRO department openly proclaimed a "case worker" approach, in which the officers viewed themselves as advocates for youths and their families within the school system. Several SROs noted that they frequently recommended more lenient treatment of students than school officials. One explained: "We got a call about a kid stealing sandwiches from the cafeteria. They [school administrators] want him arrested. We get there and talk to the kid and hear that he hasn't eaten since yesterday. . . . We're not going to arrest in those situations."

2. The decision to arrest or issue a court summons to a student rather than to use traditional school disciplinary measures is often based on subjective and inconsistent reasoning.

The factors that determine whether a student is referred to a clerk magistrate or a juvenile judge or subject only to school discipline are often defined by an officer's personality, a youth's demeanor and attitude, and the extent of pressure put on the SRO by school officials. Several officers also told us that they made arrest decisions based on what they knew about the student's family background and history.

We also found that school officials often turn to law enforcement when they don't have other counseling or mental health services available to serve troubled students. For example, one officer justified arresting a ten-year-old boy for continuing to open the front door after he had been told repeatedly not to do so. "What else was there for me to do? I had to arrest him. He was driving the A.P. berserk."

3. Officers maintain that placing SROs in the school building rather than relying on a "call-for-service" model reduces the number of school-based arrests over time.

The SROs we interviewed in almost every district strongly insisted that when a police officer operating on a call-for-service basis relies solely on a school administrator's characterization of an incident, the likelihood of arrest of a student is higher than if an SRO is permanently placed in the school. They maintained that in schools where an SRO is a daily presence and member of the school community, the SRO, students, and administrators become more comfortable with one another, and arrests decrease, sometimes dramatically. Unfortunately, we were unable to confirm these claims because of a lack of accurate data on school-based arrests in these districts. One article, authored by Matthew Theriot, both supports and refutes this contention. Theriot found that in the schools he studied, the presence of an SRO does reduce arrests for serious offenses, such as assaults and weapons possession, but increases arrests for the more subjective offense of "disorderly conduct," which can be broadly applied to a wide array of behaviors.[17]

4. Officers' lack of training is highly problematic.

Many officers take courses offered by the National Association of School Resource Officers (NASRO), but these are not required by the state or district. Moreover, NASRO instruction tends to emphasize technical training, such as the deployment of security devices and cameras within schools. The officers with whom we spoke did not receive training in mediation, basic de-escalation techniques, or in detecting symptoms and behaviors of youths who have been exposed to violence, trauma, or abuse. They rarely had formal understanding of adolescent psychology or knowledge about the legal protections extended to youths on individual education plans.

5. There is little internal or external oversight of the work of SROs or examination of their overall effects on school climate.

The lack of interest in collecting accurate or detailed data about school-based arrests and court referrals by most police and school departments was striking. This gap in information makes it extremely difficult to contest or verify police claims about reductions in school-based arrests over time. It also leaves them vulnerable to claims that they are overarresting or arresting in a biased manner. In most schools, neither SROs nor school officials give formal notification to parents and students of the scope of their role and powers in school-based activities or students' due process rights. In some schools, SROs and school officials meet regularly. In others, the relationship between police and school officials is entirely informal and focused only on incidents.

RECOMMENDATIONS FOR REFORMS

The following recommendations are predicated upon our acknowledgment that school resource officers have become an accepted part of most schools. Thus, we put forth suggestions that we believe will maximize the benefits and "resources" derived from their continued involvement in schools.

1. Schools and SROs should clearly define the consequences of certain behaviors and communicate those consequences to students and parents.

In particular, they should identify those behaviors that may lead to arrest or court summons. Youths rarely understand, or are even aware of, the law and the consequences of their conduct. Indeed, officers often reported to us that students held many incorrect assumptions about criminal law and legal process. Further, in view of the level of discord among adults (including teachers, administrators, SROs, and the courts) about how to treat certain behaviors, it is clear that such distinctions are highly subjective and no doubt confusing to youths.

We recommend that school districts closely follow the approach now in place in Denver, Colorado; Clayton County, Georgia; and Birmingham, Alabama public schools. In those systems, an agreement has been worked out by all parties and communicated to students and parents that law enforcement intervention will be limited to certain offenses. Greater clarity about what conduct will lead to an arrest in a school may also empower youths and their parents to observe and challenge how the law and discipline are implemented in their schools.

2. The federal and state departments of education should mandate better and more comprehensive data collection.

The inadequacy of the data collected on school arrests and court referrals is nothing short of shameful. Given the potentially devastating effect of pushing youths into the juvenile justice system and frequent accusations of "frivolous" or inappropriate school-based arrests, it is critical that detailed and comprehensive data be kept by both the schools and the police about law enforcement intervention in school-based incidents. These data should include the age, race, sex, grade, and disability status of any student who is arrested or summoned to appear in court; a brief description of the incident precipitating the arrest; the name of the arresting officer; and the school official or teacher who pressed for the arrest or summons.

3. School districts should mandate community oversight.

A major weakness that we identified in most SRO programs is the lack of oversight of the use of police in school generally and officers' actions specifically. Many SROs are dedicated professionals, who provide help and resources to students. Nonetheless, too much discretion has been built into their jobs, which raises the very real risk that some SROs will target certain students for harsher penalties than others. Without appropriate oversight, the same applies for school officials, who may choose to use law enforcement intervention to "push out" certain students.

Thus, while maintaining confidentiality of individual students, we recommend that a community board that includes parents, youth advocates, and social service providers regularly review all school-based incidents leading to law enforcement intervention to ensure that no racial profiling or inappropriate targeting of certain students is occurring.

4. States and districts should require more and better training for SROs.

School resource officers who interact daily with students—some of whom are deeply troubled—and who make decisions that will profoundly affect their lives need knowledge and training regarding (a) adolescent development and psychology; (b) strategies for diffusing potentially volatile situations; (c) recognizing symptoms of poverty, trauma, abuse, and exposure to violence; (d) recognizing manifestations of students' disabilities protected under federal and state laws; and (e) the short- and long-term effects of court involvement, including detention, on the likelihood of recidivism and disengagement from school. Many SROs possess strong instinctive and empathic understanding of the students with whom they interact. This needs to be augmented with the latest and most current knowledge about adolescent psychology and development. These types of training are particularly important for SROs working in schools with large numbers of youths of color, immigrant youth, and youths living in poverty.

5. Schools should replace zero tolerance with graduated sanctions and implement programs aimed at addressing root causes of student misbehaviors.

Schools should implement interventions and programs, such as the Positive Behavioral Interventions Systems and restorative justice practices, that replace zero tolerance with graduated sanctions and that aim to address root causes of student misbehaviors. Research clearly shows that students feel more "connected" to schools when they perceive discipline as fair and tolerant.[18] A student's sense of connection to school is associated with a host of positive outcomes, including reduced likelihood of engaging in violence or substance abuse, or becoming pregnant.

CONCLUSION

Absent drastic cuts in police departments, SROs are likely to remain permanent fixtures in schools. In most districts, they enjoy strong external support. At least one study has confirmed that their presence seems to reduce the number of serious incidents, such as weapons possession, that occur in schools. At the same time, there is an inherent danger in allowing a law enforcement approach to adolescent misbehavior to trump an educational perspective. Police are trained to view certain incidents, such as shoving matches or food fights, as potentially dangerous or violent, where educators may see opportunities for the "teachable moment."

Referring a student to juvenile court or arresting him in school should be an action of last resort, made only when the student is a danger to himself or to the school community. Such actions can permanently derail a student's academic future, put her at risk of dropping out, and increase the likelihood that she will be pushed deeper into the criminal justice system. These encounters often traumatize youths and isolate them from the school community during a developmental period when their greatest need is for connections with healthy peers and adults.

Currently, youths are arrested too often in school because of larger systemic failures on the part of adults to create positive learning climates; provide mental health and health services; or offer adequate training to teachers, school resource officers, and other school officials. These failures can be rectified. Our recommendations are designed to ensure that the best aspects of the SRO programs—the feelings of comfort and security that they provide to parents and communities, the reduction in serious crimes, and the caring relationships that many develop with students—are maintained, while the potential for abuse and unnecessary criminalization of vulnerable students is reduced.

NOTES

13. See Andrew Block and Virginia Weisz, "Choosing Prisoners over Pupils," the *Washington Post*, July 6, 2004, A-19.

14. Estimate from the National Association of School Resource Officers (NASRO) See www.nasro.org.

15. See, for example, Lisa H. Thurau and Johanna Wald, "Controlling Partners: When Law Enforcement Meets Discipline in Public Schools." www .nyls.edu/user_files/1/3/4/17/49/1001/Thurau%20&%20Wald%2054.4.pdf.

16. See, for example, studies on Toledo's "safe school ordinance," by Victor Goode, and on effects of new "disrupting public schools" law, by Jennifer Obidah, presented at the 2003 Civil Rights Project conference on the School to Prison Pipeline. Available online at www.charleshamiltonhouston.org. Judith Browne, of the Advancement Project, was quoted in an article in the *Nation*: "We're seeing very minor conduct becoming a criminal act. Things a police officer might not arrest someone for in a bar fight, we're seeing schools calling in police to make arrests for. . . . It could be a student who refuses to sit down in class, or the spitball," she said. "In addition to getting the three-to-five-day suspension, these kids are getting arrested" ("Discipline and Punish: Zero tolerance policies have created a 'lockdown environment' in schools," by Annette Fuentes, the *Nation*, December 15, 2003).

17. Matthew T. Theriot, "School Resource Officers and the Criminalization of Student Behavior," *Journal of Criminal Justice* 37(3) (May–June 2009), pp. 280–287.

18. Clea A. McNeely, James M. Nonnemaker, and Robert W. Blum, "Promoting School Connectedness: Evidence from the National Longitudinal Study of Adolescent Health," *Journal of School Health* 72(4) (April 2002), pp. 138–146. Available online at http://www2.gsu.edu/~wwwche/ Promoting%20School%20Connectedness%20Evidence%20from%20the%20 Natl%20Longitudinal%20Study%20of%20Adolescent%20Health.pdf.

PURSUING THE PROMISE OF *BROWN* IN THE TWENTY-FIRST CENTURY

by Erica Frankenberg

Erica Frankenberg's published work on integration and the U.S. public school system is widely known within the field and offers a fine overview of critical issues that must be engaged if the United States is to be successful in achieving meaningful public school integration. Her essay here reframes the challenges of Brown v. Board of Education *in the advent of color-blind racial politics and the unprecedented racial transformation of U.S. public school populations—both urban and suburban—from majority white institutions into multiracial majorities, including Latino populations. Frankenberg notes that Latino populations were not accorded the right to desegregation by the Supreme Court until 1973 and that as a racial group, continue to experience rising levels of segregation from white populations to the present day. Frankenberg outlines a three-point strategy to viably pursue integration in the context of these transforming racial demographics and the failure of recent educational policies (e.g., the former Bush administration's No Child Left Behind Act) to apply both equity- and achievement-based institutional approaches.*

Many commentators recognize the 1954 *Brown v. Board of Education* decision by the U.S. Supreme Court as being among the most monumental events of the twentieth century, launching both the civil rights movement and a number of other social movements that asserted rights for groups historically marginalized in the United States. Despite the *Brown* decision's declaration that segregated schools were unconstitutional, our nation's public schools have become increasingly segregated over the last several decades. Ironically, since the time of the *Brown* decision, we have learned much more about the ways in which segregation limits students' life opportunities and how integration benefits students of all races. Our efforts to achieve public school integration in the twenty-first century will have to be three dimensional:

(1) reclaim the focus and language of the civil rights movement, (2) update for multiracial public school enrollment, and (3) spread beyond urban areas to our nation's booming suburban communities. While schools alone cannot integrate all aspects of our society, without attending to all three dimensions, our progress toward truly achieving the vision of *Brown* will be halting and incomplete.

The first decade after *Brown* saw relatively little movement in ending the rigid system of racially separate schools in seventeen states and the District of Columbia. Yet, in the mid- to late 1960s in the South, dramatic progress toward school desegregation was made through the combined efforts of local civil rights advocates and the executive and legislative branches of the federal government to bring cases, require enforcement of court orders, and negotiate desegregation settlements in countless numbers of school districts across the region. By 1970, the South was the most integrated region of the country for black students and remained so for thirty-five years.

Since 1970, active integration efforts have ended. The number of court-ordered desegregation cases have dwindled dramatically after the Supreme Court's decisions in 1990 limited what was required of districts to be declared fully desegregated, and most recently, the Supreme Court limited even *voluntary* (i.e., not court ordered) efforts at integrating students. As the Supreme Court has moved from being desegregation champion to foe, the focus of educational reform has also shifted from equity to excellence. While the two goals—equity and excellence—aren't mutually exclusive, in a society with deep residential segregation, a lack of explicit attention on school desegregation has unsurprisingly coincided with a rise in segregation. As school choice has grown in popularity, access to school choice has been framed as the new civil rights issue, which overlooks the fact that one of the most popular forms of choice, charter schools, is a sector of schools with extremely high levels of minority isolation and with a disturbing percentage of schools that show little evidence of offering the subsidized lunch program, which is essential for allowing many low-income families to choose such schools. Refocusing on integration in the midst of these legal and policy trends is essential if we are to reverse the current trend of growing segregation.

Second, student enrollment—even in the South, which was the focus of desegregation efforts decades ago—is vastly different from what it was during the civil rights movement. The percentage of white students has declined dramatically due to lower white birthrates and immigration. The public school student enrollment in 2007–2008 is only 56 percent white and is projected to become majority non-white in the next generation of students. Latino students are now the second-largest group of students, at 21 percent—a group for whom the Supreme Court didn't even recognize the right to desegregation until 1973, after the most active period of implementing desegregation had ended. As a result, Latinos have experienced rising segregation from whites since the late 1960s. Black students, historically the focus of most desegregation efforts, remain concentrated in the South and in urban districts, while the share of Asian students also grows rapidly. What's more, some of these newer minority groups have considerable diversity *within* them. Generational status, English language acquisition, and country of origin can portend significant differences within the larger racial classifications commonly used.

This blossoming diversity should urge us—as the Supreme Court did in 2007—to rethink what a "diverse" school is. What counts as a segregated school? How do you pursue integration where three or more racial groups exist in significant numbers, as is the case in a growing number of communities? These questions are vital to grapple with, especially as our teaching force and schools of education that prepare teachers and educational leaders remain overwhelmingly white.

Third, in addition to developing more racially complex understanding of segregation and integration, it is also important to broaden the geographic scope of how we think about integration. Diversity is rapidly spreading into formerly homogeneous suburban regions. The racial composition of students attending suburban schools in our nation's twenty-five largest metropolitan areas mirrored that of the overall student enrollment, as more than 40 percent of these students were non-white. Just this decade, nearly 70 percent of the growth of suburban students in these largest metros has been that of Latinos, while conversely, the percentage of white students in the suburbs is falling. Further, as we see the number of poor students growing (a trend that preceded our recent national economic crisis), the majority of these students are enrolling in suburban schools.

Yet, as the suburban schools diversify, there is little focus on issues of segregation, and far too often suburban schools are replicating patterns of segregation found in central cities. An earlier study found that more than one-third of black and Latino students were attending racially isolated minority schools or schools that had fewer than 10 percent of students who were white. Such schools are often of concentrated poverty. Within suburbia itself, segregation exists between suburban districts. There are districts whose enrollment looks more similar to traditional notions of suburbia (overwhelmingly white, low poverty), while there are other districts with growing numbers of two or more minority groups in suburban districts with little prior experience or present understanding of integration between schools or practices to promote equity and integration within schools.

This issue of between-district segregation is especially significant in metropolitan areas in the Northeast and Midwest, where suburbia comprises *hundreds* of small school districts and where racial and economic segregation is, consequently, extremely high. Rethinking schooling on a more regional, metropolitan level, as is done in many areas of the South, for example, could help to address such segregation, improve the educational experiences of students, and may even be cost effective.

More than five decades after the *Brown* decision, in which the Supreme Court decisively stated that separate schools were not equal, we struggle to implement this vision in our nation's public schools, which remain one of our *only* arenas in which people of different races all participate. Continuing to strive for integration and equity in the twenty-first century—values that an overwhelming percentage of Americans say they believe are important for schools—must be renewed. To do so will require attention from all levels of government and the support of educators. It must be reconsidered on a multiracial metropolitan basis, and it must be done to provide opportunity to all and to prepare citizens and workers for their future in a multiracial democracy and economy.

NOTES

1. For an insightful discussion of the relation between structural racism and the "culture of segregation," see Douglas S. Massey and Nancy A. Denton, *American Apartheid: Segregation and the Making of the Underclass* (Cambridge, Mass.: Harvard University Press, 1993), pp. 148–185. Also, see Michael Omi and Howard Winant, *Racial Formation in the United States: From the 1960s to the 1990s* (New York: Routledge, 1994), pp. 54–55. We would also reject the language of "pathology" (see Chapter 1, note 2) in describing the cultural and/or psychological conditions of urban underclass communities, on the grounds that such vocabularies lend themselves to biological interpretations and are rarely applied to white communities in relation to social practices that sustain racial inequality (e.g., Arizona's recent anti-immigration law is supported by most white populations in the state on the basis of "border security"). This view elides the fact that the bill itself was drafted by a lawmaker, Kris Kobach, who served as a member/lawyer for the Federation for American Immigration Reform, which the Southern Poverty Law Center, since 2007, has listed as a "hate group." See Eugene Robinson, "Border security isn't the problem," in the *Washington Post*, May 4, 2010, A-23; and "Hate Group Lawyer Drafted Arizona's Anti-Immigrant Law," from the Southern Poverty Law Center's Hatewatch website at www.splcenter.org.

2. See, for example, Jonathan Kozol's *The Shame of the Nation: The Restoration of Apartheid Schooling in America* (New York: Crown, 2005).

3. For an excellent overview, see "Looking to the Future—Legal and Policy Options for Racially Integrated Education in the South and the Nation," a national conference on the *PICS* case convened at the Center for Civil Rights at the University of North Carolina School of Law, on April 2, 2009.

4. Justice Kennedy's "controlling opinion" prevented a "majority," though not "plurality," opinion here, which nonetheless was sufficient to outlaw the voluntary integration plans of both the Seattle and Louisville school districts. While Kennedy, however, supported most of the Roberts opinion, he did significantly write that "a district may consider it a compelling interest to achieve a diverse student population" (see Josh Bassett and Erica Frankenberg, "Parents Involved in Community Schools v. Seattle School District: A Social Science and Semiotic Analysis," unpublished essay prepared for the Kirwan Institute for the Study of Race and Ethnicity's Kirwan *Transformative Race* conference, Columbus, Ohio, November 30–December 2, 2007). Also, see the responses of

both the Kirwan Institute for the Study of Race and Ethnicity and the Civil Rights Project/Proyecto Derechos Civiles to the *PICS* case on their websites at http://civilrightsproject.ucla.edu/ and www.kirwaninstitute .org/, respectively.

5. Incredibly, and we do not apply this description lightly, Roberts extends his argument of "racial balancing" to assert that the Seattle and Louisville school districts' efforts to promote integrated school popula-tions are legally indistinguishable from the efforts of school districts *prior to Brown v. Board of Education* to sustain segregation: "What do the racial classifications do in these cases, if not determine admission to a public school on a racial basis? Before *Brown*, schoolchildren were told where they could or could not go to school based on the color of their skin. The school districts in these cases have not carried the heavy burden of demonstration that we should allow this once again. . . . The way to stop discriminating on the basis of race is to stop discriminating on the basis of race" (Roberts, Section IV, *PICS*). Justice Clarence Thomas, in his own opinion of Roberts's argument, affirms this specious equivalence by writing, "What was wrong in 1954 cannot be right today" (Thomas, p. 33).

6. See, for example, Patricia Gurin, Eric. L. Dey, Sylvia Hurtado, and Ger-ald Gurin's article, "Diversity and Higher Education: Theory and Impact on Educational Outcomes," *Harvard Educational Review* 72(3) (Fall 2010), pp. 330–366; and Patrick T. Terenzini, Alberto F. Cabrera, Carol L. Colbeck, Ste-fani A. Bjorklund, and John M. Parente's article, "Racial and Ethnic Diversity in the Classroom: Does It Promote Student Learning?" *The Journal of Higher Education* 72(5) (September/October 2001), pp. 509–530. Also, note an of-ficial statement by the Association of American Universities, endorsed by the presidents of sixty-two research universities: "We speak first and foremost as educators. We believe that our students benefit significantly from education that takes place within a diverse setting" (Terenzini et al., "Racial and Ethnic Diversity in the Classroom," p. 510).

7. This mitigation of the historical effects of structural racism and/ or its contemporary manifestations in educational, economic, and social spheres represents what Bonilla-Silva has identified as the color-blind frame of "minimization of racism," which also functions to privilege class conditions over race in explaining urban inequality, including segregation (Eduardo Bonilla-Silva, *Racism Without Racists: Color-Blind Racism and the Persistence of Racial Inequality in the United States*, New York: Rowman & Littlefield, 2006, pp. 43–49). Also, note Omi and Winant's critique of this model: "Racial dynamics must be understood as determinants of class

relationships and indeed class identities, not as mere consequences of these relationships" (*Racial Formation in the United States*, pp. 34, 24–35).

8. See "Still Separate, Still Unequal," by Samuel G. Freedman, the *New York Times: Sunday Book Review*, May 16, 2004.

9. See Chungmei Lee and Erica Frankenberg, "A Multiracial Society With Segregated Schools: Are We Losing the Dream?" Civil Rights Project at the University of California at Los Angeles (UCLA), January 16, 2003. See www.civilrightsproject.ucla.edu.

10. We have developed a model project here in Detroit for such a program. See Josh Bassett, "Transforming the U.S. into a true multiracial democracy," at Race-Talk.org (a Kirwan Institute project), May 27, 2010. See www.race-talk.org/?p=4542.

11. See Gary W. Gallagher and Alan T. Nolan, *The Myth of the Lost Cause and Civil War History* (Bloomington: Indiana University Press, 2000).

12. This paper is adapted from a policy brief titled "First, Do No Harm," written by the authors and released in April 2010 by the Charles Hamilton Houston Institute for Race and Justice.

For notes 13 through 18, please see p. 125.

6

MULTIRACIAL DEMOCRACY
and the Urban Crisis

The concept of multiracial democracy has been familiar to university and related academic institutions for well over a decade[1] but remains little known to the general public. In our view, the concept is likely to be regarded as superfluous by many white populations (and non-whites as well) who subscribe to color-blind views that race plays no relevant role in sustaining America's urban crisis. Many white populations hold specious ideas that the United States has become a "post-racial"[2] society and accordingly would view the concept of a multiracial democracy as yet another example of minority communities seeking to impose, through the agenda of "political correctness,"[3] their own views of American identity upon the majority of U.S. populations.

Though color-blind discourse certainly represents an improvement over its preceding era of scientific racism, wherein whites were considered to be intellectually superior to non-whites, its opposition to race consciousness practices that are necessary to redress historical structural racial inequalities and, indeed, disavowal that such inequalities are today linked to race demand that the concept of multiracial democracy be recognized as a goal for a nation founded on the principle of human equality.

The basis of this argument ties to the development of American democracy itself and the now commonplace critical recognition that for virtually all of its history, the United States has severely limited the access of its populations on the basis of race (and obviously gender and class) to participation in a democratic government and society.[4] Contemporary color-blind views minimize this history and instead advance the position that, while however flawed, the project of American democracy has been fulfilled as an ideal that is inclusive to all races. While we certainly affirm the idea that democracy itself must be racially inclusive, the presumption that this has been achieved is what we reject. We believe that laying claim to the language of race in the form of multiracial democracy is necessary to contest this view. The color-blind thesis that posits that democracy by its very nature includes racial equality ignores how racialized our democratic system of government has operated. Michael Omi and Howard Winant have importantly noted that while the United States has functioned as a democracy on certain dimensions, it has also functioned as a racial dictatorship[5] for most of its history, wherein racial identity proved determinative to equality. Adherence to the concept of the United States solely as democracy subsumes this history and the sustaining ways in which racial dynamics produce inequalities, while reframing our concept of democracy in racial terms (i.e., a multiracial democracy recognizes the distinct histories and related conditions of racial populations in the United States, and the project that yet remains before the nation is to achieve racial equality).

The concept of multiracial democracy, particularly as iterated within educational discourse (e.g., in civics/history/social studies courses, etc.), can also enhance our understanding of race itself as a social construction and the historical processes by which racial hierarchies/regimes have developed and influence contemporary practices of segregation. Moreover, directly linking the concept of race to democracy can provide insight into how language and representations function to construct racial stereotypes, which is critical to understanding questions of why certain racial groups are privileged over one another. Such examples include the case of residential housing preferences or in terms of identifying key dynamics of racial categories, for example, widely accepted critical studies of whiteness that theorize white identity secures its power in the United States by disavowing its linkage to any association of privilege.[6]

It is for these reasons, and its inherent opposition to color-blind ideology, that the concept of a multiracial democracy be recognized as an egalitarian objective of the nation. The following essays offer further elucidation of this project.

IN OUR LIFETIME[7]

by Henry Louis Gates, Jr.

Gates's essay offers a poignant analysis of the unprecedented election of Barack Obama as the first African American president of the United States and what this signifies in the context of liberative events within black American history. His discussion of the structural forms of racism that have contained black populations and their responses to this marginalization provides valuable insight into the frequent contradictory sociopolitical views that still exist between blacks and whites. He also shows how these structural forms of racism influence our very national dialogue on race, which so far, has failed to develop a common vocabulary necessary to respond to enduring racial inequalities in the United States, as well as to the realization of a multiracial democracy.

Again, as we have emphasized, the advent of the Obama administration represents profound racial progress, but as demonstrated via substantial color-blind efforts to define his election as irrefutable proof that racism no longer meaningfully exists in the United States, the peril is that key civil rights objectives that have not materialized for more than half a century will remain unaddressed or overturned (as in three recent Supreme Court cases concerning integration, voting rights, and affirmative action).[8] We are hopeful, however, as the triumphant tone of Gates's essay reflects, that President Obama will in fact effectively engage these civil rights issues appropriately, that is, outside the influence of color-blind ideology. Certainly the administration's creation of the White House Office of Urban Affairs, which will push forward a national urban agenda[9] that has otherwise been neglected for decades, represents an important development to this end.

From toiling as White House slaves, to President-elect Barack Obama, we have crossed the ultimate color line.

A new dawn of American leadership is at hand.

President-elect Barack Obama.

We have all heard stories about those few magical transformative moments in African American history, extraordinary ritual occasions through which the geographically and socially diverse black community—a nation within a nation, really—molds itself into one united body, determined to achieve one great social purpose and to bear witness to the process by which this grand achievement occurs.

The first time was New Year's Day, in 1863, when tens of thousands of black people huddled together all over the North waiting to see if Abraham Lincoln would sign the Emancipation Proclamation. The second was the night of June 22, 1938, the *storied rematch between Joe Louis and Max Schmeling*, when black families and friends crowded around radios to listen and cheer as the Brown Bomber knocked out Schmeling in the first round. The third, of course, was Aug. 28, 1963, when the Rev. Dr. Martin Luther King Jr. *proclaimed to the world that he had a dream*, in the shadow of a brooding Lincoln, peering down on the assembled throng, while those of us who couldn't be with him in Washington sat around our black-and-white television sets, bound together by King's melodious voice, through our tears and with quickened-flesh.

But we have never seen anything like this. Nothing could have prepared any of us for the eruption (and, yes, that is the word) of spontaneous celebration that manifested itself in black homes, gathering places, and the streets of our communities when Sen. Barack Obama was declared President-elect Obama. From Harlem to Harvard, from Maine to Hawaii—and even Alaska—from "the prodigious hilltops of New Hampshire . . . [to] Stone Mountain of Georgia," as Dr. King put it, each of us will always remember this moment, as will our children, whom we woke up to watch history being made.

My colleagues and I laughed and shouted, whooped and hollered, hugged each other and cried. My father waited 95 years to see this day happen, and when he called as results came in, I silently thanked God for allowing him to live long enough to cast his vote for the first black man to become president. And even he still can't quite believe it!

How many of our ancestors have given their lives—how many millions of slaves toiled in the fields in endlessly thankless and mindless labor—before this generation could live to see a black person become president? "How long, Lord?" the spiritual goes. "Not long!" is the resounding response. What would Frederick Douglass and W. E. B. Du Bois say if they could know what our people had at long last achieved? What would Sojourner Truth and Harriet Tubman say? What would Dr. King himself say? Would they say that all those lost hours of brutalizing toil and labor leading to spent, half-fulfilled lives; all those humiliations that our ancestors had to suffer through each and every day; all those slights and rebuffs and recriminations; all those rapes and murders, lynchings, and assassinations; all those Jim Crow laws and protest marches, those snar'ing dogs, and bone-breaking water hoses; all of those beatings and all of those killings; all of those black collective dreams deferred—that the unbearable pain of all of those tragedies—had, in the end, been assuaged at least somewhat through Barack Obama's election? This certainly doesn't wipe that bloody slate clean. His victory is not redemption for all of this suffering; rather, it is the symbolic culmination of the black freedom struggle, the grand achievement of a great, collective dream. Would they say that surviving these horrors, hope against hope, was the price we had to pay to become truly free, to live to see—exactly 389 years after the first African slaves landed on these shores—that "great gettin' up morning" in 2008, when a black man—Barack Hussein Obama—was elected the first African American president of the United States?

I think they would, resoundingly and with one voice proclaim, "Yes! Yes! And yes, again!" I believe they would tell us that it had been worth the price that we, collectively, have had to pay—the price of President-elect Obama's ticket.

On that first transformative day, when the Emancipation Proclamation was signed, Frederick Douglass, the greatest black orator in our history before Martin Luther King Jr., said that the day was not a day for speeches and "scarcely a day for prose." Rather, he noted, "it is a day for poetry and song, a new song." Over 3,000 people, black and white abolitionists together, waited for the news all day in Tremont Temple, a Baptist church a block from Boston Common. When a messenger burst in, after 11 p.m., and shouted, "It is coming! It is on the wires," the church went mad; Douglass recalled that "I never saw enthusiasm before. I never saw joy." And then he spontaneously led the crowd in singing "Blow Ye the Trumpet, Blow," John Brown's favorite hymn:

> Blow ye the trumpet, blow!
> The gladly solemn sound
> Let all the nations know,
> To earth's remotest bound:
> The year of jubilee is come!
> The year of jubilee is come!
> Return, ye ransomed sinners, home.

At that moment, an entire race, one that in 1863 in the United States comprised 4.4 million souls, became a unified people, breathing with one heart, speaking with one voice, united in mind and spirit, all their aspirations concentrated into a laser beam of almost blind hope and desperate anticipation.

It is astounding to think that many of us today—myself included—can remember when it was a huge deal for a black man or woman to enter the White House through the front door, and not through the servants' entrance. Paul Cuffe, the wealthy sea captain, shipping merchant, and the earliest "Back to Africa" black colonist, will forever have the distinction of being the first black person to be invited to the White House for an audience with the president. Cuffe saw President James Madison at the White House on May 2, 1812, at precisely 11 a.m. and asked the president's intervention in recovering his famous brig *Traveller*, which had been impounded because officials said he had violated the embargo with Britain. Cuffe, after the Quaker fashion, called Madison "James"; "James," in turn, got Paul's brig back for him, probably because Cuffe and Madison both favored the emigration of freed slaves back to Africa. (Three years later, on Dec. 10, 1815, Cuffe used this ship to carry 38 black people from the United States to Sierra Leone.)

From Frederick Douglass, who visited Lincoln three times during his presidency (and every president thereafter until his death in

1895), to Sojourner Truth and Booker T. Washington, each prominent black visitor to the White House caused people to celebrate another "victory for the race." Blacks became frequent visitors to Franklin Roosevelt's White House; FDR even had a "Kitchen Cabinet" through which blacks could communicate the needs of their people. Because of the civil rights movement, Lyndon Johnson had a slew of black visitors, as well. During Bill Clinton's presidency, I attended a White House reception with so many black political, academic, and community leaders that it occurred to me that there hadn't been as many black people in the Executive Mansion perhaps since slavery. Everyone laughed at the joke, because they knew, painfully, that it was true.

Visiting the White House is one thing; occupying the White House is quite another. And yet, African American aspirations to the White House date back generations. The first black man put forward on a ticket as a political party's nominee for U.S. president was George Edwin Taylor, on the National Liberty Party ticket in 1904. Portions of his campaign document could have been written by Barack Obama:

> In the light of the history of the past four years, with a Republican president in the executive chair, and both branches of Congress and a majority of the Supreme Court of the same political faith, we are confronted with the amazing fact that more than one-fifth of the race are actually disfranchised, robbed of all the rights, powers and benefits of true citizenship, we are forced to lay aside our prejudices, indeed, our personal wishes, and consult the higher demands of our manhood, the true interests of the country and our posterity, and act while we yet live, 'ere the time when it shall be too late. No other race of our strength would have quietly submitted to what we have during the past four years without a rebellion, a revolution, or an uprising.

The revolution that Taylor goes on to propose, he says, is one "not by physical force, but by the ballot," with the ultimate sign of the success being the election of the nation's first black president.

But given all of the racism to which black people were subjected following Reconstruction and throughout the first half of the 20th century, no one could actually envision a Negro becoming president—"not in our lifetimes," as our ancestors used to say. When James Earl Jones became America's first black fictional president in the 1972 film, *The Man*, I remember thinking, "Imagine that!" His character, Douglass Dilman, the president pro tempore of the Senate, ascends to the presidency after the president and the speaker of the House are killed in a building collapse, and after the vice president declines the office due to advanced age and ill health. A fantasy if ever there was one, we thought. But that year, life would imitate art: Congresswoman Shirley Chisholm attempted to transform "The Man" into "The Woman," becoming the first black woman to run for president in the Democratic Party. She received 152 first-ballot votes at the Democratic National Convention. Then, in 1988, Jesse Jackson got 1,219 delegate votes at the Democratic convention, 29 percent of the total, coming in second only to the nominee, Michael Dukakis.

The award for prescience, however, goes to Jacob K. Javits, the liberal Republican senator from New York, who, incredibly, just a year after the integration of Central High School in Little Rock, predicted that the first black president would be elected in the year 2000. In an essay titled "Integration from the Top Down" printed in *Esquire* magazine in 1958, he wrote:

> What manner of man will this be, this possible Negro Presidential candidate of 2000? Undoubtedly, he will be well-educated. He will be well-traveled and have a keen grasp of his country's role in the world and its relationships. He will be a dedicated internationalist with working comprehension of the intricacies of foreign aid, technical assistance and reciprocal trade. . . . Assuredly, though, despite his other characteristics, he will have developed the fortitude to withstand the vicious smear attacks that came his way as he fought to the top in government and politics . . . those in the vanguard may expect to be the targets for scurrilous attacks, as the hate mongers, in the last ditch efforts, spew their verbal and written poison.

In the same essay, Javits predicted both the election of a black senator and the appointment of the first black Supreme Court justice by 1968. Edward Brooke was elected to the Senate by Massachusetts voters in 1966. Thurgood Marshall was confirmed in 1967. Javits also predicted that the House of Representatives would have "between thirty and forty qualified Negroes" in the 106th Congress in 2000. In fact, there were 37 black U.S. representatives, among them 12 women.

Sen. Javits was one very keen prognosticator. When we consider the characteristics that he insisted the first black president must possess—he must be well-educated, well-traveled, have a keen grasp of his country's role in the world, be a dedicated internationalist and have a very thick skin—it is astonishing how accurately he is describing the background and character of Barack Obama.

I wish we could say that Barack Obama's election will magically reduce the numbers of teenage pregnancies or the level of drug addiction in the black community. I wish we could say that what happened last night will suddenly make black children learn to read and write as if their lives depended on it, and that their high school completion rates will become the best in the country. I wish we could say that these things are about to happen, but I doubt that they will.

But there is one thing we can proclaim today, without question: that the election of Barack Obama as president of the United States of America means that "The Ultimate Color Line," as the subtitle of Javits' *Esquire* essay put it, has, at long last, been crossed. It has been crossed by our very first postmodern Race Man, a man who embraces his African cultural and genetic heritage so securely that he can transcend it, becoming the candidate of choice to tens of millions of Americans who do not look like him.

How does that make me feel? Like I've always imagined my father and his friends felt back in 1938, on the day that Joe Louis knocked out Max Schmeling. But ten thousand times better than that. All I can say is "Amazing Grace! How sweet the sound."

MAKING EVERY VOTE COUNT[10]

by Lani Guinier

Though Guinier's essay concerns the 2000 presidential election between George W. Bush and Al Gore, we include it in our collection because it foregrounds the need for a national engagement in the project of multiracial democracy, as well as examines the role of race in what many consider to be an illegitimate electoral outcome that was determined by a conservative majority of the U.S. Supreme Court rather than the actual votes of the citizens of Florida.[11] Guinier argues that if we are to achieve a multiracial democracy, then the Electoral College must be transformed from a "winner-take-all" system to one that accounts for substantial numbers of voters whose ballots should have relevance even if their candidate fails to garner a majority of votes, as is the case in Maine and Nebraska.

To further support this position, Guinier outlines the historical origins of the Electoral College, which were motivated by racist political structures of the South related to the infamous "three-fifth's compromise," which counted individual slaves as three-fifths of a human being for electoral purposes. In modern politics, the call for electoral reform in the nation has been all but universally rejected by the Republican Party for decades, until the election of Barack Obama, where significant GOP political efforts were taken to parcel the ballots of California in ways that would account for actual electoral votes in heavily Republican districts.[12] That such a dramatic change in policy position was driven by the election of the nation's first African American, or more specifically, bi-racial president, in the context of the nation's unprecedented racial demographic transformation, highlights the need for extensive discussions of the nature of multiracial democracy and, obviously, the implementation of civic policies that will ensure U.S. voters are not marginalized (via the prison-industrial complex, voting rights obstructions, or other means) in any elections.

For years, many of us have called for a national conversation about what it means to be a multiracial democracy. We have enumerated the glaring flaws inherent in our winner-take-all form of voting, which has produced a steady decline in voter participation, under-representation of racial minorities in office, lack of meaningful competition and choice in most elections, and the general failure of politics to mobilize, inform, and inspire half the eligible electorate. But nothing changed. Democracy was an asterisk in political debate, typically encompassed in a vague reference to "campaign finance reform." Enter Florida.

The fiasco there provides a rare opportunity to rethink and improve our voting practices in a way that reflects our professed desire to have "every vote count." This conversation has already begun, as several highly educated communities in Palm Beach experienced the same sense of systematic disfranchisement that beset the area's poorer and less-educated communities of color.

"It felt like Birmingham last night," Mari Castellanos, a Latino activist in Miami, wrote in an e-mail describing a mammoth rally at the 14,000-member New Birth Baptist Church, a primarily African American congregation in Miami. "The sanctuary was standing room only. So were the overflow rooms and the school hall, where congregants connected via large TV screens. The people sang and prayed and listened. Story after story was told of voters being turned away at the polls, of ballots being destroyed, of NAACP election literature being discarded at the main post office, of Spanish-speaking poll workers being sent to Creole precincts and vice-versa. . . . Union leaders, civil rights activists, Black elected officials, ministers, rabbis, and an incredibly passionate and inspiring Marlene Bastiene—president of the Haitian women's organization—spoke for two or three minutes each, reminding the assembly of the price their communities had paid for the right to vote and vowing not to be disfranchised ever again.

We must not let this once-in-a-generation moment pass without addressing the basic questions these impassioned citizens are raising: Who votes, how do they vote, whom do they vote for, how are their votes counted, and what happens after the voting? These questions go to the very legitimacy of our democratic procedures, not just in Florida but nationwide—and the answers could lead to profound but eminently achievable reforms.

WHO VOTES—AND DOESN'T?

As with the rest of the nation, in Florida only about half of all adults vote, about the same as the national average. Even more disturbing, nonvoters are increasingly low-income, young, and less educated. This trend persists despite the Voting Rights Act, which since 1970 has banned literacy tests nationwide as prerequisites for voting—a ban enacted by Congress and unanimously upheld by the Supreme Court.

We are a democracy that supposedly believes in universal suffrage, and yet the differential turnout between high-income and low-income voters is far greater than in Europe, where it ranges from 5 to 10 percent. More than two-thirds of people in America with incomes greater than $50,000 vote, compared with one-third of those with incomes under $10,000. Those convicted of a felony are permanently banned from voting in Florida and twelve other states. In Florida alone, this year more than 400,000 ex-felons, about half of them black, were denied the opportunity to vote. Canada, on the other hand, takes special steps to register former prisoners and bring them into full citizenship.

HOW DO THEY VOTE?

Florida now abounds with stories of long poll lines, confusing the voting booth. The shocking number of invalid ballots—more ballots were "spoiled" in the presidential race than were cast for "spoiler" Ralph Nader—are a direct result of antiquated voting mechanics that would shame any nation, let alone one of the world's oldest democracies. Even the better-educated older voters of Palm Beach found, to their surprise, how much they had in common with more frequently disfranchised populations. Given how many decisions voters are expected to make in less than five minutes in the polling booth, it is common sense that the polls should be open over a weekend, or at least for twenty-four hours, and that Election Day should be a national holiday. By highlighting our wretched record on voting practices, Florida raises the obvious question: Do we really want large voter participation?

WHOM DO THEY VOTE FOR?

Obviously, Florida voters chose among Al Gore, George Bush, and a handful of minor-party candidates, who, given their status as unlikely to win, were generally ignored and at best chastised as spoilers. But as many voters are now realizing, in the presidential race they were voting not for the candidates whose name they selected (or attempted to select) but for "electors" to that opaque institution, the Electoral College. Our constitutional framers did some things well—chiefly dulling the edge of winner-take-all elections through institutions that demand coalition-building, compromise, and recognition of certain minority voices—but the Electoral College was created on illegitimate grounds and has no place in a modern democracy.

As Yale law professor Akhil Reed Amar argues, the Electoral College was established as a device to boost the power of Southern states in the election of the president. The same "compromise" that gave Southern states more House members by counting slaves as three-fifths of a person for purposes of apportioning representation (while giving them none of the privileges of citizenship) gave those states Electoral College votes in proportion to their Congressional delegation. This hypocrisy enhanced the Southern states' Electoral College percentage, and as a result, Virginia slave owners controlled the presidency for thirty-two of our first thirty-six years.

Its immoral origins notwithstanding, the Electoral College was soon justified as a deliberative body that would choose among several candidates and assure the voice of small geographic areas. But under the Electoral College, voters in small states have more than just a voice; indeed their say often exceeds that of voters in big states. In Wyoming one vote in the Electoral College corresponds to 71,000 voters; in Florida, one electoral vote corresponds to 238,000 voters. At minimum we should eliminate the extra bias that adding electors for each of two senators gives our smallest states, as Robert Naiman of the Center for Economic and Policy Research reports. Allowing each state only as many electors as it has members in the House of Representatives would mean, for example, that even if Bush won Oregon and Florida, he would have 216 and Gore would have 220 electoral votes.

Today its backers still argue that the Electoral College is necessary to ensure that small states are not ignored by the presidential candidates. Yet the many states—including small ones—that weren't close in this election were neglected by both campaigns. Some of the nation's biggest states, with the most people of Color, saw very little presidential campaigning and get-out-the-vote activity. Given their lopsided results this year, we can expect California, Illinois, New York, Texas, and nearly all Southern states to be shunned in the 2004 campaign.

HOW ARE THEIR VOTES COUNTED?

The presidency rests on a handful of votes in Florida because allocation of electoral votes is winner-take-all—if Gore wins by ten votes out of 6 million, he will win 100 percent of the state's twenty-five electoral votes. The ballots cast for a losing candidate are always "invalid" for the purposes of representation; only those cast for the winner actually "count." Thus winner-take-all elections underrepresent the voice of the minority and exaggerate the power of one state's razor-thin majority. Winner-take-all is the great barrier to representation of political and racial minorities at both the federal and the state level. No blacks or Latinos serve in the U.S. Senate or in any governor's mansion [2000 statistics]. Third-party candidates did not win a single state legislature race except for a handful in Vermont.

Given the national questioning of the Electoral College sparked by the anomalous gap between the popular vote and the College's vote in the presidential election, those committed to real representative democracy now have a chance to shine a spotlight on the glaring flaws and disfranchisement inherent in winner-take-all practices and to propose important reforms.

What we need are election rules that encourage voter turnout rather than suppress it. A system of proportional representation—which would allocate seats to parties based on their proportion of the total vote—would more fairly reflect intense feeling within the electorate, mobilize more people to participate, and even encourage those who do participate to do so beyond just the single act of voting on Election Day. Most democracies around the world have some form of proportional voting and manage to engage a much greater percentage of their citizens in elections. Proportional representation in South Africa, for example, allows the white Afrikaner parties and the ANC to gain seats in the national legislature commensurate with the total number of votes cast for each party. Under this system, third parties are a plausible alternative. Moreover, to allow third parties to run presidential candidates without being "spoilers," some advocate instant-runoff elections (IRVs—currently adopted for local elections in San Francisco and Oakland) in which voters would rank their choices for president. That way, even voters whose top choice loses the election could influence the race among the other candidates.

Winner-take-all elections, by contrast, encourage the two major parties to concentrate primarily on the "undecideds" and to take tens of millions of dollars of corporate and special-interest contributions to broadcast ads on the public airwaves appealing to the center of the political spectrum. Winner-take-all incentives discourage either of the two major parties from trying to learn, through organizing and door-knocking, how to mobilize the vast numbers of disengaged poor and working-class voters. Rather than develop a vision, they produce a product and fail to build political capacity from the ground up.

WHAT HAPPENS AFTER THE VOTING?

Our nation is more focused on elections now than it has been for decades; yet on any given Sunday, more people will watch professional football than voted this November. What democracy demands is a system of elections that enables minor parties to gain a voice in the legislature and encourages the development of local political organizations that educate and mobilize voters.

Between elections, grassroots organizations could play an important monitoring role now unfulfilled by the two major parties. If the Bush campaign is right that large numbers of ballots using the same butterfly format were thrown out in previous elections in Palm Beach, then something is wrong with more than the ballot. For those Democratic senior citizens in Palm Beach, it was not enough that their election supervisor was a Democrat. They needed a vibrant local organization that could have served as a watchdog, alerting voters and election officials that there were problems with the ballot. No one should inadvertently vote for two candidates; the same watchdog organizations should require ballot-counting machines like those in some states that notify the voter of such problems before he or she leaves the booth. Voters should be asked, as on the popular TV quiz show, "Is that your final answer?" And surely we cannot claim to be a functioning democracy when voters are turned away from the polls or denied assistance in violation of both state and federal law.

Before the lessons of Florida are forgotten, let us use this window of opportunity to forge a strong pro-democracy coalition to rally around "one vote, one value." The value of a vote depends on its being fairly counted but also on its counting toward the election of the person the voter chose as her representative. This can happen only if we recognize the excesses of winner-take-all voting and stop exaggerating the power of the winner by denying the loser any voice at all.

SEGREGATION BY RACE, SEGREGATION FROM OPPORTUNITY, AND THE SUBVERSION OF MULTIRACIAL DEMOCRACY IN DETROIT

by Andrew Grant-Thomas

In considering key barriers to the achievement of a viable multiracial democracy, Andrew Grant-Thomas's essay focuses on the question of how spatial geographies—neighborhoods, in particular—become racialized and the consequences of this racialization for a community's economic opportunities and its social and race relations. Grant-Thomas applies the critical methodology of "opportunity mapping" to show that in Detroit, African Americans and Latinos are far more likely to inhabit "low-opportunity" areas than are their white counterparts. Grant-Thomas offers examples of what this structural inequality of opportunity means for residents' quality of life, for civic attitudes and race relations, and for democratic processes and outcomes. His essay is a call for greater attention to segregation by race and segregation from social opportunity.

Grab a map of Detroit, plunk your finger down right in the middle of it, and you just might land on the historic Boston-Edison neighborhood. Automaker Henry Ford, baseball great Ty Cobb, and businessman Sebastian S. Kresge are among the many prominent whites who historically have called those thirty-nine city blocks home. Today, Detroit is a predominantly African American city—an estimated 82 percent black in 2008[13]—and so is Boston-Edison. Detroit is also famously segregated. Demographer William Frey's analysis of the 2005–2009 American Community Survey found that blacks and whites in metropolitan Detroit are more segregated from each other residentially than their counterparts in all of the country's 100 largest metro regions, with the exception of Milwaukee.[14] And so, too, is Boston-Edison.

Start with the block bounded by Glynn Court to the north and Linwood Avenue to the west. Ninety-nine percent of the people who live in that block are African American.[15] Move south to the adjacent block. One hundred percent of its residents are black. Next block, 97 percent black. Next one, 94 percent black. Last block on the western border of Boston-Edison, 99 percent black. Very few residents of Boston-Edison are Latino or Asian American. The few "white" blocks are clustered in the far eastern portion of the area. They are 71 percent white, 62 percent white, 43 percent white, 38 percent white, and 24 percent white. In very few of the remaining blocks does the percentage of white neighbors rise above the low single digits. In Boston-Edison, as in much of Detroit, segregation operates within neighborhoods as well as across them.

Why does this tight relationship between race and place matter? It matters because social burdens and opportunities typically interconnect in, and often vary substantially across, lived space. "Opportunity mapping" is an analytical tool that allows us not only to assess the landscape of opportunity across a particular location—a neighborhood, a Census tract, a region—but also to compare how populations of interest are positioned within that geography of opportunity. Using 2000 Census data and fifteen indicators spanning the areas of education, employment, and neighborhood quality, the Kirwan Institute mapped opportunity across the Detroit metropolitan area.[16] We found that nine in ten African Americans and six in ten Latinos—compared to only two in ten whites—lived in low-opportunity areas.

Consider what this deeply racialized access to place-based opportunities meant for children in Detroit's three largest racial/ethnic groups. It meant that the average black or Latino child lived in a poorer neighborhood than the average poor white child (24 percent, 17 percent, and 14 percent, respectively).[17] It meant that black children attended elementary schools where three-quarters of their peers were poor, and half the students were poor in schools attended by Latino children. At their white counterparts' schools, one in five students was poor. We have a mountain of research studies that testify to the corrosive effects high school-poverty rates have on individual student achievement.[18] It meant that most children of color had little access to supermarkets and the fresh, healthy, affordable produce they provide.[19] Indeed, variations in neighborhood life and quality have been linked repeatedly to a range of health outcomes, including "mortality, general health status, disability, birth outcomes, chronic conditions, health behaviors and other risk factors for chronic disease, as well as with mental health injuries, violence and other important health indicators."[20] It is clear that poor, racially isolated neighborhoods exact a terrible toll on the people who live in them.

What does all this have to do with multiracial democracy? How does the correspondence between racial segregation and opportunity segregation relate to the capacity and willingness of ordinary people to engage each other and their leaders to participate effectively in the decisions that shape the conditions of their lives? For one, the racially disparate conditions apparent throughout the Detroit landscape expose the gap between the governance system we have and the multiracial democracy we often regard ourselves to be.

At a meeting of civic engagement groups in Washington, D.C., some years ago, I noted to the director of a leading citizen engagement organization that all our talk at the meeting had focused on questions of process—how to get representative groups of stakeholders around key decision-making tables and how to empower them once there. Shouldn't we also be talking about the fairness of the decisions such groups might reach, I wondered. Wasn't democracy about equitable outcomes as well as representative inputs? The director replied that in all her years of doing civic engagement work, she had found that well-constituted, informed groups always arrived at good decisions that supported the collective. Whether equitable outcomes are a central concern or merely a derivative benefit of truly democratic practices, the pernicious interaction between race and opportunity in the city and throughout the region itself suggests that multiracial democracy remains more aspiration than reality.

The congruence between racial and opportunity segregation also has direct implications for democratic practice and civic engagement. A functioning democracy relies substantially on trust, and particularly on trust that extends beyond immediate and relatively small circles of families and friends. It is trust that allows us to engage in collective action for the public good and, more generally, makes us willing to submit to a system of governance in which many decisions that affect our personal and family welfare are made or endorsed by strangers. In a multiracial society, that "generalized" trust must also extend across racial lines. However, in resource-poor, disordered neighborhoods, such as the ones that many Latino and black Detroiters call home, residents are likely to distrust strangers, and neighbors are likely to distrust each other.[21] Where distrust is high, civic life withers. The correspondence between racial and opportunity segregation also means that social problems associated with place readily become associated with race. Under such circumstances, African Americans—and Latinos, to a lesser degree—become racialized in especially derogatory ways. For example, a recent study found that whites in Chicago and Detroit regard all-black and racially mixed neighborhoods as much less attractive than identical neighborhoods with white residents alone.[22] Put differently, the mere "presence of African Americans in a neighborhood resulted in a downgrading of its desirability." A *Washington Times* story on racial tensions in Detroit summarized it this way: "Whites say their neighbors consider blacks to be violent and solely responsible for problems in the black community. Blacks say many of their own consider whites to be spoiled and condescending."[23] No wonder that in 2009, two in three Detroit metro-area residents acknowledged being divided by race and income.[24] Certainly, this divisiveness does not bode well for the realization of multiracial democracy.

So whither the "Arsenal of Democracy," as Franklin D. Roosevelt in 1940 dubbed Detroit? In September 2010, in the face of huge and ongoing economic decline, population losses, and budgetary shortfalls, Mayor Dave Bing launched the Detroit Works project to engage city residents in an effort to plan the city's future. Downsizing the city and severely restricting public services to its most sparsely populated areas to save on costs are explicit expectations. There have been widespread complaints about the mayor's outreach process and fears expressed about its possible irrelevance to his administration's decision making. Of course, that such a high-stakes process would provoke consternation is hardly surprising, regardless of how well or unfairly the engagement and decision-making process goes.

My hope for Mayor Bing and the people of Detroit is that they prove able to draw lessons from the aftermath of Hurricanes Katrina and Rita throughout the Gulf Coast and from the recent Great Recession. In both cases, as in economically devastated Detroit, communities already marginalized by race, poverty, and geography were the ones hardest hit. In both cases, we learned that there is no such thing as a natural disaster. Similarly, local, state, and federal policies were as culpable in bringing the city to its knees as they can yet be helpful in forging an effective path forward. As with the Gulf Coast and the recession, in Detroit too we must understand that "recovery" should mean more than restoring the status quo. It must mean that we "build back better," dismantling the apparatus of racial segregation, narrowing the equity gap, and promoting greater opportunity for all Detroiters.

NOTES

13. "Races in Detroit, Michigan (MI) Detailed Stats: Ancestries, Foreign born residents, place of birth," City-Data.com, accessed January 18, 2011, at www.city-data.com/races/races-Detroit-Michigan.html.

14. "New Racial Segregation Measures for States and Large Metropolitan Areas: Analysis of the 2005–2009 American Community Survey," Census Scope, accessed January 18, 2011, at http://censusscope.org/ACS/Segregation.html.

15. "Boston-Edison neighborhood in Detroit, Michigan (MI), 48202, 48206 detailed profile," City-Data.com, accessed January 18, 2011, at www.city-data.com/neighborhood/Boston---Edison-Detroit-MI.html.

16. Jason Reece, Christy Rogers, john a. powell, and Andrew Grant-Thomas, "Opportunity for All: Inequity, Linked Fate and Social Justice in Detroit and Michigan" (paper presented at the Michigan Roundtable for Diversity and Inclusion, Detroit, Michigan, July 2008). Available online at

http://4909e99d35cada63e7f757471b7243be73e53e14.gripelements.com/ publications/MI_Roundtable_Full_report.pdf.

17. "Detroit-Warren-Livonia, MI Profile: Residential Integration and Neighborhood Characteristics," The DiversityData project, accessed January 18, 2011, at http://diversitydata.sph.harvard.edu/Data/Profiles/Show. aspx?loc=420&notes=True&rgn=None&cat=5.

18. John Charles Boger, "Education's 'Perfect Storm?': Racial Resegregation, 'High States' Testing & School Inequities: The Case of North Carolina" (paper submitted to the University of North Carolina's conference on "The Resegregation of Southern Schools?: A Crucial Moment in the History (and the Future) of Public Schooling in America," Chapel Hill, North Carolina, August 30, 2002). See www.uncpress.unc.edu/browse/book_detail?title _id=1373.

19. Shannon N. Zenk, PhD, Amy J. Schulz, PhD, Barbara A. Israel, DrPH, Sherman A. James, PhD, Shuming Bao, PhD, and Mark L. Wilson, "Neighborhood Racial Composition, Neighborhood Poverty, and the Spatial Accessibility of Supermarkets in Metropolitan Detroit," *American Journal of Public Health* 95(4), 2005, pp. 660–667.

20. Catherine Cubbin, Veronica Pedregon, Susan Egerter, and Paula Braveman, "Where We Live Matters for Our Health: Neighborhoods and Health," Robert Wood Johnson Foundation Commission to Build a Healthier America, Issue Brief 3 (2008) at www.rwjf.org/files/research/commissionneighborhood102008.pdf.

21. Sandra Susan Smith, "Race and Trust," *Annual Review of Sociology* 36 (2010). Also, the 2000 Social Capital Community Survey concluded that "southeast Michigan residents fall slightly short of national averages in terms of trusting their neighbors and people of other races." See www.cfsv .org/communitysurvey/mi5c.html.

22. Maria Krysan, Mick P. Couper, Reynolds Farley, and Tyrone A. Forman, "Does Race Matter in Neighborhood Preferences?: Results from a Video Experiment," *American Journal of Sociology* 115(2), 2009, pp. 527–559.

23. "Detroit's racial divide colors debate," the *Washington Times*, October 7, 2008, accessed January 18, 2011, at www.washingtontimes.com /news/2008/oct/07/detroits-racial-divide-colors-debate/.

24. The Kaiser Family Foundation, "Survey of Detroit Area Residents," accessed January 18, 2011, at www.kff.org/kaiserpolls/upload/8039.pdf.

HOW WE ARE WHITE[25]

by Gary Howard

Howard's essay, which derives from his decades of experience in both developing multiracial educational curricula and teaching in multiracial classrooms, offers crucial insight into one of the key structural mechanisms that sustains color-blind ideology and related politics and their ineffectiveness in responding to contemporary racial inequalities and urban crisis conditions. This structural mechanism is based on the construction of white identity and how populations throughout U.S. history who have been defined as white have been privileged in civic, economic, and social capacities over non-white communities. Though many whites (and non-whites, as well) perceive racial identity as natural, it is, as noted, a social construction[26] that has been variously applied to human beings primarily in the interests of power and subjugation. For example, Noel Ignatiev[27] has documented in his classic study how Irish immigrant populations, who were initially not considered white in the early history of the United States, became identified as white in later periods through a combination of social and civic processes. Howard examines these processes in contemporary terms and argues that for the United States to achieve a multiracial democracy, whites must become aware of their whiteness in opposition to color-blind discourse that otherwise renders invisible their racial identity and privileged group position within America.

The break is over and I am ready to begin the second half of a four-hour multicultural curriculum workshop. Twenty-five teachers and staff are scrunched into second grade desks, all eyes and white faces turned toward their one African American colleague, who has asked to address the group. He announces that he will be leaving this workshop immediately and resigning at the end of the year. He has lost hope in their willingness and ability to deal with issues of race.

After he leaves, a painful silence grips the room. I realize that my planned agenda is no longer appropriate. Gradually the participants begin to talk. Their comments are rife with guilt, shame, anger, blame, denial, sadness, and frustration. It becomes clear there has been a long history leading to this moment. Together they are experiencing a collective meltdown over the realities of race and their own whiteness. One faculty member remarks, "I feel so helpless. What am I supposed to do as a white teacher?"

In my thirty-five years of work in multicultural education, I have encountered a seemingly universal uneasiness about race among white educators. Since the publication of my book, *We Can't Teach What We Don't Know: White Teachers, Multiracial Schools* (Teachers College Press, 1999, 2006), many people have shared their stories with me. A white teacher from California reports, "I realize that I have contributed to the failure of my students of color by not being able to drop the mask of privilege that I wear." Another white teacher writes, "I thought I was going crazy. It was helpful to hear that other white teachers feel similar confusion."

As white educators, we are collectively bound and unavoidably complicit in the arrangements of dominance that have systematically favored our racial group over others. In my own family, the farm in Minnesota that I cherish as part of our heritage was actually stolen from the Ojibwe people only a few years before my great-grandparents acquired it. This is only one of the countless ways I am inextricably tied to privilege. I did not personally take the land, yet I continue to benefit from its possession.

But privilege and complicity are only part of the story. The police officers who brutally assaulted civil rights activists during the first Selma march in 1965 were certainly white but so were some 500 of the marchers who stood on the Edmund Pettus Bridge two days later with Dr. Martin Luther King, Jr. to protest the violence of that bloody Sunday. It is true that three white men dragged James Byrd to a horrific death in Jasper, Texas, but it is also true that many white townspeople and a predominantly white jury condemned this act of racist violence.

In the course of my work and personal reflection, I have discovered there are many ways of being white. Some whites are bound by a *fundamentalist white orientation*. They view the world through a single lens that is always right and always white. White supremacist hate groups represent one particularly hostile form of fundamentalist white identity, while the Tea Party version masks its racism under the guise of patriotism. They self-righteously flaunt the flag and the constitution under the banner of "I want my country back," which more accurately translates as "I want to keep the White House white." Yet another form of fundamentalist white identity exists, an uninformed and well-intentioned version that simply has never been exposed to other perspectives nor questioned its own. This was my orientation from birth through my high school years, when I had never met a person who wasn't white. Fundamentalist white teachers often say things like "I don't see color," or "I treat all my students the same," or "Why are they sending *those* kids to *our* school?"

Other white folks live from an *integrationist white orientation*, where differences are acknowledged and tolerated but still not fully accepted, appreciated, or respected. Integrationist whites are self-congratulatory in their apparent openness to racial differences, yet often paternalistic and condescending toward people of color. In this way of being white, we prefer to keep the peace, avoid confrontation, and maintain control rather than actually get to the core of our separate truths and unique racial perspectives. Integrationist white teachers say to students of color "I know how you feel," even when we have no real connection to their reality. This was my orientation when I first began "helping" black kids in the ghetto in the 1960s. I thought I was the solution rather than the problem. Related to the work of eliminating racial achievement gaps, educators in the integrationist orientation often put the blame on our students of color and their parents rather than questioning how our own beliefs and practices might be contributing to the educational disparities we see manifested in our classrooms.

Third is the *transformationist white orientation*, which is a place of humility and active engagement in one's own continuing growth and reformation. Transformationist whites have acquired a paradoxical identity, which allows us to acknowledge our inevitable privilege and racism while at the same time actively work to dismantle our legacy of dominance. Transformationist white teachers know it is our place and our responsibility to engage issues of race and social justice in the classroom. We become allies and advocates for our students and colleagues of color and antiracist change agents among our white colleagues. We know that the real work of school reform requires us to transform both ourselves and our practices and to challenge the arrangements of dominance that underpin school inequities. Transformationist white educators know that policies like No Child Left Behind and Race to the Top are tragically inadequate to address the deeply rooted social justice and racial disparities that continue to fuel school failure for far too many of our students of color.

White educators do have a choice to grow beyond our ignorance, denial, and guilt. Throughout the country and over many years, I continue to meet transformationist white educators who have made that clear choice and that deep commitment to continue to work and grow personally and professionally in racially diverse schools rather than flee to the white enclaves of suburbia. There is a journey for us, which I envision like a river that carries us through many confusing currents and treacherous rapids, but which eventually can lead to a place of authentic multicultural white identity. Ultimately, good teaching is not a function of the color of our skin. It is much more closely related to the temperament of our mind and the hue of our heart. We did not choose whether to be white, but we can effect how we are white. This is both our challenge and our hope.

In the last few years, I have returned several times to work with the elementary staff who experienced such a painful meltdown over issues of race. With courage, they have stayed on the river, chosen to look deeply into the reflective pool of their own difficult history together, and have come to a place of greater honesty and renewed commitment to a multicultural vision for their school. At our last meeting, when the painful event was alluded to in discussion, a newly hired Asian-American teacher asked, "What happened?" A veteran white teacher responded, "It's a long story we need to share with you. It will help you know who we are."

NOTES

1. See Lani Guinier's comments on multiracial democracy in her essay in Chapter 6 of this book, "Making Every Vote Count." Also, see Lani Guinier and Pamela Karlan, "Confirmative Action in a Multiracial Democracy in the State of Black America" (presentation at the National Urban League in 2000); Cornel West, *Race Matters* (Boston: Beacon Press, 2001); Henry Giroux, "Schooling for Critical Citizenship," *Synthesis/Regeneration* 5 (Winter 1993).

2. See, for example, Thomas J. Sugrue, *Not Even Past: Barack Obama and the Burden of Race* (Princeton, N.J.: Princeton University Press, 2010).

3. Robert Stam and Ella Shohat offer an important analysis of "political correctness" in their influential work, *Unthinking Eurocentrism* (New York: Routledge, 2000), pp. 340–346.

4. Howard Zinn's *A People's History of the United States* remains a classic text here (New York: HarperCollins, 2000).

5. "For most of its existence both as a European colony and an independent nation, the U.S. was a *racial dictatorship*. From 1607 to 1865—258 years—most non-whites were firmly eliminated from the sphere of politics. . . . In [this] wake followed almost a century of legally sanctioned segregation . . . [whose] barriers fell only in the mid-1960s" (Michael Omi and Howard Winant, *Racial Formation in the United States: From the 1960s to the 1990s*, New York: Routledge, 1994, pp. 65–66).

6. Academic literature here is abundant. For a fine survey, see Paula S. Rothenberg's *White Privilege: Essential Readings on the Other Side of Racism* (New York: Worth, 2005).

7. This article originally appeared on www.theroot.com on November 5, 2008.

8. These cases are *Parents Involved in Community Schools v. Seattle School District No. 1* (see Chapter 5 in this book), *Bartlett v. Strickland* (which restricted the Voting Rights Act in North Carolina), and *Ricci v. DeStefano* (which rejected affirmative action policies regarding firefighters in Connecticut).

9. Robin Shulman, "White House to Push Forward on National Urban Policy Agenda," the *Washington Post*, July 12, 2009.

10. Reprinted with permission from the December 4, 2000, issue of the *Nation* magazine. For subscription information, call 1-800-333-8536. Portions of each week's *Nation* magazine can be accessed at www.thenation.com.

11. See, for example, Alan M. Dershowitz's *Supreme Injustice: How the High Court Hijacked Election 2000* (New York: Oxford University Press, 2001).

12. "Republicans want share of California electoral votes," *CNN.com/ Politics*, August 9, 2007. See http://articles.cnn.com/2007-08-09/politics/ california.split_1_electoral-votes-winner-take-all-system-electoral-college?_s=PM:POLITICS.

For notes 13 through 24, please refer to pages 154–55.

25. This article is an edited version of an article that originally appeared on Teaching Tolerance (www.tolerance.org). Reprints of the original article can be obtained from www.tolerance.org.

26. As, noted, Omi and Winant offer an important analysis here via their concept of "racial formation" (*Racial Formation in the United States*, pp. 53–76).

27. Noel Ignatiev, *How the Irish Became White* (New York: Routledge, 1995).

7

TOWARD SOLUTIONS
to the Urban Crisis

In assessing the status of America's urban crisis some forty years after the historic Kerner Commission Report was issued in response to the civil rebellions that swept across cities throughout the United States in the 1960s, Edward W. Brooke, one of the report's original authors, concluded the following: "The core conditions that the Kerner Commission identified as key to civil unrest are as prevalent, if not as virulent, today as they were 40 years ago."[1]

This sobering assessment has been made even more problematic by the fact that in the initial period, when the Kerner Report was issued, racism and racial discrimination were highly visible features of American society, which stood in such contradiction to the nation's democratic ideals, that millions of Americans collectively engaged in an historic struggle for civil rights. Today, however, the influence of color-blind discourse has nearly reduced this engagement to a personal level and rendered structural racial inequalities merely as consequences of group behavior and by-products of cultural differences.

We have emphasized the paramount need to challenge the primacy of color-blind ideology as a means to begin to develop both a common vocabulary of race, through which we can arrive at a more beneficial understanding of race relations, and specific civic policies that can begin to redress the nation's enduring urban inequalities, which until the recent election of Barack Obama as president of the United States, seemed consigned to intractable neglect.

In outlining what we feel are practical solutions to this crisis that can be implemented at local, state, and national levels, we believe the four major urban revitalization strategies, as conceived by Farley, Danziger, and Holzer (Chapter 1)—labor market supply strategies, mobility strategies, labor market demand strategies, and anti-discrimination strategies—provide an excellent framework through which to transform urban inequalities and move America closer to multiracial democracy. These strategies, which are detailed in Farley, Danziger, and Holzer's book, *Detroit Divided*, taken together with newly emerging efforts to revitalize afflicted urban areas through community-based agriculture and economic enterprises (e.g., those currently being implemented in Detroit),[2] can provide viable avenues of racial integration to areas that have otherwise remained racially polarized despite significant demographic changes in racial populations.

From our own efforts undertaken in Detroit, we would also foreground in Farley and colleague's strategic paradigms the role of multiracial education and the development of new collaborative models of public education. We feel these paradigms can be developed in numerous dimensions to respond to the structural and representational foundations of racism and discrimination in the United States.

Specifically, we propose—following models that we have established in Detroit and its metro-suburban areas—an unprecedented collaborative relationship among high schools, community colleges, and universities, wherein all three entities share educational resources in the implementation of service-learning-based dual/concurrent enrollment programs. Such a collaborative relationship would allow high school students from otherwise racially segregated areas to participate in diverse classes/programs to enhance racial understanding, facilitate community engagement, and most importantly, allow students to earn transferable college credits that are directly tied to higher-education programs designed to enhance student achievement at the college/university level.

We believe, and have preliminary data to support,[3] that this kind of collaborative educational model can engender related initiatives, wherein students engage their own schools, parents and community groups, and civic entities, among others, in efforts to challenge racial stereotypes and promote programs that will begin to help equalize the massive racial and economic disparities that continue to produce great harm to the nation as a whole. Importantly, as is the case with emerging urban residential initiatives, this multi-institutional collaboration can also provide viable sites of integration to persistently segregated racial geographies.

These educational and economic efforts—coordinated with the need for obvious reforms in the U.S. criminal justice system (e.g., policies of mass incarceration, reformation of drug laws, adoption of restorative justice, and creation of effective reentry programs, etc.), changes in lending/banking practices, and reforms in key areas outlined in this book—in our view, offer viable interventions that can be implemented on even moderate scales, with a positive impact for America's urban communities, which continue to live in urban crisis conditions.

The choice of whether we continue to live as two nations, separate and unequal, is ours.

NOTES

1. See Edward W. Brooke, "King and Kerner: An Unfinished Agenda," the *Washington Post*, April 3, 2008, A-17.
2. See, for example, Christine MacDonald, "Summit to focus on Detroit's future size, shape," the *Detroit News*, May 12, 2010.
3. Data collection conducted in coordination with the Kirwan Institute for the Study of Race and Ethnicity.

INDEX

powell, john, 85
presidential elections: campaigns
    by blacks, 140–41; 2000, 143–49
President's Initiative on Race, 25
prisoners: Pell grants for, 61, 67;
    population tied to state legisla-
    ture and politics, 26
prison-industrial complex, xii, 17,
    32; costs of, 61; key areas of, 54
prison system: costs of, 54; evolu-
    tion of, 71. *See also* incarceration
profiiing. *See* racial profiling
proportional voting, 148
Proposition 209 (civil rights initia-
    tive, California), 57–58
public good, 153
Pulp Fiction (film), 39

race(s): Arizona's race and ethnic
    studies ban, 50n6; conscious-
    ness, 45, 133; displacement and,
    34–35; drugs and, 62, 81n3;
    grid of differentiation and, 31;
    hierarchies of, 9, 84, 101n10,
    134; incarceration and, 53,
    61–62, 71–74, 81n1, 102n13;
    intelligence and, 9, 11–12; lan-
    guage of, 24, 49n2; One America
    national conversation about, 95;
    problems, views on, 39; religious
    definition of, 11; representation,
    semiotic theory and, 36, 50n10;
    scientific and biological defini-
    tion of, 12, 22, 25–26; as social
    and political construction, 12,
    15–16; as social category, 25–26;
    social conditions and, xii
Race (Terkel), 40
race card, in politics, 26

race relations: calls for dialogue on,
    xvii; color-blind policies' impact
    on, 17, 113; in Detroit, 8–9;
    improvements in, xv, 163
Race to Incarcerate (Mauer), 71
Race to the Top, 159
racial advantages, types of, 29
racial awareness, epochs in evolu-
    tion of, 11–12
racial balancing, 104, 131n5
racial categories, 27, 134
racial demographic information,
    26–27
racial dictatorship, U.S. as, 134,
    160n5
racial differences, 12; whites and,
    36–37
racial discrimination, xv, 4; residen-
    tial, 4–5
racial diversity, 104, 128–29, 159
*Racial Formation in the United
    States: From the 1960s to the
    1990s* (Omi and Winant), 10–16
racial formation theory, 2, 15–16, 21
racial identity: color-blind perspec-
    tive of, 12–13; stereotypes of, 5,
    9, 19n6, 134; views of, 103, 156
racial integration. *See* integration
racially-mixed neighborhoods in
    Chicago, 153
racial politics, color-blind era of, xv,
    xviii, 11–15
racial power, 27–30
Racial Privacy Initiative (Califor-
    nia), 27, 50n8
racial profiling: in courts, 62; im-
    prisonment of mentally ill and,
    75–77; Magbie and, 78–81; MWB
    and, 32; war on terror and, 45, 47

racial projects, 16, 21
racial sameness, in media, 36–41
racial segregation: opportunity segregation and, 152–53; outlawing
of, 56. *See also* segregation
racial superiority, xv
racism: blacks and, 31–32; color-
blind, 21, 57, 59–60; color-blind
ideology, multiracial democracy
and, 24–30, 133–34; conceptual
deflation of, 27; cultural, 19n2,
22; definition of, 29; in Detroit,
32; hate and, 24, 28; history
of, 31–32; laissez-faire, 55, 56;
minimization of, 22, 84, 131n7;
scientific, 55, 133; structural,
50n7, 56, 59–60, 131n7, 136;
whites on, 115
racist acts as crimes of passion, 28
Reagan, Ronald, 11, 13
Reagan Administration, xii, 13; integration and, 97; war on drugs
and, 53
"Rebuilding Lives: Restoration,
Reformation, and Rehabilitation in the U.S. Criminal Justice
System" conference, 1
Reconstruction, 24, 140
reforms: campaign finance, 144; in
criminal justice system, 165; in
Detroit police department, 49;
for police in schools, 121–23
residential racial discrimination,
4–5
residential segregation: in Detroit,
7–9, 85–87, 150–54; health care
and, 88
restorative justice, 66, 67, 123
Retchin, Judith, 78

reverse discrimination, 13, 14
Roberts, Chief Justice, 103–4,
131n5
Roosevelt, Franklin D., 140, 153
Rosenblatt, Roger, 40
Rust Belt, 3, 32

Schmeling, Max, 137, 142
school resource officers (SROs),
117–24; call-for-service model
and, 120; case worker approach
by, 119; training for, 120–21, 123
schools: charter, 100, 127; community control of, 106; desegregation of, 15, 88, 101n12, 127–28;
failing, 99, 106, 108, 117, 159;
Freedom, 110; police in, 117–24;
private, 98; racial diversity in,
104, 128–29, 159; suburban,
urban and rural, 98–99, 128–29;
two systems for, 98–99, 103. *See
also* education
school-to-prison pipeline, 18, 117,
118–19
scientific racism, 55, 133
Seattle, Washington, 97, 103–4,
130n4, 131n5
segregation, 83–102; declining
rates of, 101n6; economic, 85,
129; education and, xiii, 2, 18,
97–100, 103–5, 126–29; health
care and, 88–89; hospitals and,
88; hypersegregation, 100n1;
impacts of, 4, 18, 94; naturalization and, 19n4, 22, 84; opportunity, 152–53; politics and, 85, 86;
social, 22, 95; urban underclass
theory on, 83, 100n2; voluntary
forms of, xvii; in Washington,

ABOUT THE CONTRIBUTORS

Houston A. Baker was born in Louisville, Kentucky. He received his bachelor's from Howard University and his master's and doctorate from the University of California at Los Angeles. He has taught at Yale, University of Virginia, University of Pennsylvania, and Duke. He is currently Distinguished University Professor and professor of English at Vanderbilt University. His awards and honors include Guggenheim and National Endowment for the Humanities Fellowships, resident fellowships at the Center for Advanced Study in the Behavioral Sciences and the National Humanities Center, and honorary degrees from a number of U.S. colleges and universities. He has served as president of the Modern Language Association of America and is the author of articles, books, and essays devoted to African-American literary criticism and theory. His book, *Betrayal: How Black Intellectuals Have Abandoned the Ideals of the Civil Rights Era*, received an American Book Award for 2009.

Joshua Bassett, co-editor, is director of the Institute for Social Progress (ISP), a nationally affiliated civil rights and educational institute, located in Detroit, Michigan. As director of the ISP, Bassett has conducted numerous civil rights efforts aimed at redressing inequalities in Detroit and metro Detroit, including work with the Kirwan Institute for the Study of Race and Ethnicity, at the Ohio

State University, and the Center for Social Inclusion (NYC). He served as executive director of the "Educational Summit: Detroit and the Crisis in Urban America" conference (broadcast nationally on C-SPAN), as well as the national "Rebuilding Lives" criminal justice conference, held in Detroit in 2004. Prior to this book, his scholarship has focused on the June 2007 Supreme Court ruling against voluntary integration programs in Seattle, Washington and Louisville, Kentucky school districts (*Parents Involved in Community Schools v. Seattle School District No. 1*), which he conducted via the Kirwan Institute. His current academic work concerns the application of semiotic theory to studies of color-blind ideology.

Dr. **Grace Lee Boggs**, born to Chinese immigrant parents in 1915, is an activist, writer, and speaker, whose seventy years of political involvement encompass the major U.S. social movements of the twentieth century: labor, civil rights, black power, Asian American, and women's and environmental justice. In 1940, she received her doctorate in philosophy from Bryn Mawr College. In the 1940s and early 1950s, she worked with West Indian Marxist historian C.L.R. James. In 1953, she came to Detroit, where she married James Boggs, African-American autoworker, labor and community activist, and writer. Working together in grassroots groups and projects, they were partners for more than forty years until James's death in July 1993.

In 1974, they co-authored *Revolution and Evolution in the Twentieth Century*, which Monthly Review Press reissued in 2008 with a fifty-page introduction by Grace. In 2011, Wayne State University Press published the *James Boggs Reader*.

Grace's autobiography, *Living for Change*, is widely used in university classes. Her latest book, with Scott Kurashige, is *The Next American Revolution: Sustainable Activism for the 21st Century*.

Besides many lifetime achievement awards, Grace has received four honorary doctorates: Wooster College, 2002; Kalamazoo College, 2007; the University of Michigan, 2009; and Wayne State University, 2010. The University of Michigan citation reads: "You have been dynamically transformative in a pivotal epoch of human history, which you have illuminated through bold activism and thoughtful writing, providing the world with inspiring reflection and vigorous calls to action. By nurturing Detroit as a city of Hope, you have brought optimism and inspiration to our state and country."

Benjamin DeMott was a member of the Amherst College English faculty from 1951 until his retirement in 1990. He was a widely respected literary critic and social commentator and was the author of more than a dozen books, including *The Imperial Middle: Why Americans Can't Think Straight About Class*, *The Trouble with Friendship: Why Americans Can't Think Straight About Race*, and *Killer Woman Blues: Why Americans Can't Think Straight About Gender and Power*. He was also a frequent essayist for popular publications, including the *Atlantic* and *Harper's*. In May 2005, the *New York Review of Books* published an essay he had written on "Reclaiming the Game: College Sports and Educational Values." DeMott died on September 29, 2005, at his home in Worthington, Massachusetts. He was eighty-one years old.

Erica Frankenberg is an assistant professor in the Department of Education Policy Studies in the College of Education at the Pennsylvania State University. Her research interests focus on racial desegregation and inequality in K–12 schools, and the connections between school segregation and other metropolitan policies. Prior to joining the Penn State faculty, she was the research and policy director for the Initiative on School Integration, at the Civil Rights Project/Proyecto Derechos Civiles at UCLA. She received her doctorate in educational policy at the Harvard University Graduate School of Education and her AB, cum laude, from Dartmouth College. She was a research assistant for the Civil Rights Project when it was at Harvard University. Projects included developing and analyzing a national survey of teachers' racial attitudes and studying the connection between school and housing segregation. Before graduate school, Ms. Frankenberg worked with a nonprofit educational foundation focused on improving the public schools in her hometown of Mobile, Alabama.

She is the co-editor of *Lessons in Integration: Realizing the Promise of Racial Diversity in America's Schools* (with Dr. Gary Orfield), published in 2007. In 2006, Frankenberg helped coordinate and write a social science statement that was signed by 553 social scientists and filed with the Supreme Court, regarding the benefits of integrated schools. Some of her Civil Rights Project work has been cited by the Supreme Court in its recent educational diversity cases, *Grutter v. Bollinger* and *Parents Involved in Community Schools v. Seattle School District No. 1*. Her work has also been published in education policy journals, law reviews, housing journals, and practitioner publications. She is currently coordinating a study of suburban racial change, funded by the Spencer Foundation.

Henry Louis Gates, Jr. serves as the Alphonse Fletcher University Professor at Harvard University, where he is director of the W.E.B. Du Bois Institute for African and African American Research. Professor Gates is an accomplished man, a literary critic, educator, scholar, writer, editor, and public intellectual with many accolades and a great deal of knowledge to share. The recipient of nearly fifty honorary degrees and many social and academic awards, Professor Gates was named by *Time* magazine as one of the "25 Most Influential Americans," in 1997.

Professor Gates is the author of several works of literary criticism, including *Figures in Black: Words, Signs and the "Racial Self"*; *The Signifying Monkey: A Theory of Afro-American Literary Theory*, and *Loose Canons: Notes on the Culture Wars*, as well as being the 1989 winner of the American Book Award. He has also authored *Colored People: A Memoir*, which traces his childhood experiences in a small West Virginia town in the 1950s and 1960s; *The Future of the Race*, co-authored with Cornel West; and *Thirteen Ways of Looking at a Black Man*. Professor Gates has edited several anthologies, including *The Norton Anthology of African American Literature* and *The Oxford Schomburg Library of Nineteenth Century Black Women Writers*. In addition, Professor Gates is co-editor of *Transition* magazine. An influential cultural critic, Professor Gates's publications include a 1994 cover story for *Time* magazine on the new black renaissance in art, as well as numerous articles for the *New Yorker*. He wrote and produced the PBS documentary, "African American Lives," the first documentary series to employ genealogy and science to provide an understanding of African-American history.

Andrew Grant-Thomas is deputy director of the Kirwan Institute. He directs the Institute's internal operations and oversees much of its U.S.-based and global justice programming. Andrew is editor in chief of the Institute's journal, *Race/Ethnicity: Multidisciplinary Global Contexts*, and director of the bi-annual *Transforming Race* conference. His substantive interests include structural racism/racialization and systems thinking, poverty, implicit bias and racial communications, race and popular culture, and multiracial alliance building.

In 1998, **Lani Guinier** became the first black woman to be appointed to a tenured professorship at Harvard Law School. Before joining the faculty at Harvard, she was a tenured professor for ten years at the University of Pennsylvania Law School. During the 1980s, she was head of the voting rights project at the NAACP Legal Defense Fund and had served in the Civil Rights Division during the Carter Administration as special assistant to then assistant attorney General Drew S. Days. She is the author of many articles and op-ed pieces on democratic theory, political representation, educational equity, and issues of race and gender. Guinier has written *The Tyranny of the Majority* (about issues of political representation); *Who's Qualified?*, written with Susan Sturm (about moving beyond affirmative action to reconsider the ways in which colleges admit all students); and *The Miner's Canary*, written with Gerald Torres (about the experience of people of color as a warning or "canary" signaling larger institutional inequities). In 1998, Guinier also published a personal and political memoir, *Lift Every Voice: Turning a Civil Rights Setback into a New Vision of Social Justice*.

Bob Herbert joined the *New York Times* as an op-ed columnist in 1993. His twice-a-week column comments on politics, urban affairs, and social trends. Prior to joining the *Times*, Mr. Herbert was a national correspondent for NBC, from 1991 to 1993, reporting regularly on the

Today Show and *NBC Nightly News.* He had worked as a reporter and editor at the *Daily News,* from 1976 until 1985, when he became a columnist and member of its editorial board. In 1990, Mr. Herbert was a founding panelist of *Sunday Edition,* a weekly discussion program on WCBS-TV in New York, and the host of *Hotline,* a weekly issues program on New York public television. He began his career as a reporter with the *Star-Ledger,* in Newark, New Jersey, in 1970. Mr. Herbert has won numerous awards, including the Meyer Berger Award, for coverage of New York City, and the American Society of Newspaper Editors Award, for distinguished newspaper writing.

Award-winning journalist and author, **Maria Hinojosa** is president of the Futuro Media Group, a nonprofit company dedicated to producing multiplatform, community-based journalism that respects and celebrates the cultural richness of the American experience. She is also managing editor and host of *Latino USA,* a weekly National Public Radio program, reporting on news and culture in the Latino community, and anchor of the Emmy Award-winning talk show *Maria Hinojosa: One-on-One,* from WGBH/La Plaza. Hinojosa was previously the senior correspondent for the Emmy Award-winning newsmagazine *NOW,* on PBS, and urban affairs correspondent for CNN. Hinojosa has received top journalism honors, including two Emmys; the Sidney Hillman Prize, honoring her social and economic justice reporting; the Ruben Salazar Communications Award, from the National Council of La Raza; the Robert F. Kennedy Award, for reporting on the disadvantaged; and the Edward R. Murrow Award, from the Overseas Press Club, for best documentary for her groundbreaking *Child Brides: Stolen Lives.* She was named one of the 100 most influential Latinos in the United States by *Hispanic Business* magazine. Her critically acclaimed memoir, *Raising Raul: Adventures Raising Myself and My Son,* was published in 1999. In 1995, she authored the book, *Crews: Gang Members Talk with Maria Hinojosa,* which is based on her award-winning NPR report.

Gary R. Howard has over thirty-five years of experience working with issues of civil rights, social justice, equity, education, and diversity, including twenty-eight years as the founder of the REACH Center for Multicultural Education, in Bellingham, Washington. He is a keynote speaker, writer, and workshop leader who travels extensively throughout the United States and Australia. Mr. Howard has provided extensive training in cultural competence and culturally responsive practice to schools, universities, social service agencies, and businesses throughout the United States and Australia. He is the author of numerous articles on race, justice, and multicultural issues and has developed collections of curriculum materials, which are being used internationally. His most recent book, *We Can't Teach What We Don't Know* (second edition, 2006), is considered a groundbreaking work, examining issues of privilege, power, and the role of white leaders and educators in a multicultural society. The central focus of Howard's current work is to lead intensive Equity Leadership Institutes, which provide educational organizations with the internal capacity to deliver high-quality professional development for social justice and systemic change.

Dr. **Curtis L. Ivery** became chancellor and CEO of Wayne County Community College District (WCCCD) on September 1, 1995 and is currently serving on the Board of Directors for the American Association of Community Colleges (AACC), where his primary focus concerns the development of national workforce and economic initiatives. As the chief executive officer, Ivery directs the five-campus, multicultural institution, serving more than 72,000 students annually, in a 550-square-mile district. Prior to becoming chancellor of WCCCD, Ivery served as vice president of instruction and acting president at Mountain View College, of the Dallas County Community College District (DCCCD). Ivery served as commissioner of Human Services for the state of Arkansas and was the first African American and the youngest appointee to the cabinet of governor Willam Clinton of Arkansas. He has written and published more than 600 articles for several weekly and monthly metropolitan newspapers across the nation.

Colbert I. "Colby" King is a weekly columnist for the *Washington Post*, specializing in urban and national affairs. His column appears on Saturdays. Before joining the *Post*'s editorial board in 1990, King worked for the State Department, serving at the U.S. embassy in Bonn; in the Senate, where he helped draft home-rule legislation for the District of Columbia; and at the World Bank, where he was U.S. executive director. He was appointed deputy editorial page editor of the *Post* in 2000, and served in that capacity until 2007. King is a regular panelist on the public affairs program, *Inside Washington*, on ABC-TV, and a regular commentator on VTOP radio, where he was awarded the 2005 Chesapeake Associated Press Broadcasters Association Award for outstanding editorial commentary. He won the Pulitzer Prize for distinguished commentary in 2003.

Arthur Levine has been president of the Woodrow Wilson National Fellowship Foundation since 2006. Previously president and professor of education at Teachers College, Columbia University, he has also been chair of the Institute for Educational Management, at the Harvard Graduate School of Education; president of Bradford College; and a senior fellow at the Carnegie Foundation for the Advancement of Teaching and the Carnegie Council on Policy Studies in Higher Education. Levine has authored scores of articles and reviews, including a series of reports on the preparation of school leaders, teachers, and education researchers. His work has appeared in such publications as the *New York Times*, the *Los Angeles Times*, the *Wall Street Journal*, *Education Week*, *Inside Higher Education*, and the *Chronicle of Higher Education*. The more recent of his two books is *Unequal Fortunes: Snapshots from the South Bronx* (with Laura Scheiber). Levine's honors include a Guggenheim Fellowship, the American Council on Education's Book of the Year Award, and nineteen honorary degrees. A member of the American Academy of Arts and Sciences, he sits on the boards of DePaul University and Say Yes to Education. He received his bachelor's degree from Brandeis University and his doctorate from the State University of New York at Buffalo.

Manning Marable, who passed away April 1, 2011, was one of America's most influential historians and political interpreters of the black experience. Marable was M. Moran Weston and Black

Alumni Council Professor of African-American Studies and professor of history, political science, and public affairs at Columbia University in New York City. From 1993 to 2003, he was founding director of Columbia's Institute for Research in African American Studies. Since 2002, he had served as director of the Center for Contemporary Black History (CCBH). CCBH publishes a quarterly academic publication, *Souls: A Critical Journal of Black Politics, Culture, and Society*, distributed by Taylor & Francis. CCBH also produces web-based educational resources, including the Ford Foundation-funded www.amistadresource.org.

Marc Mauer is the executive director of the Sentencing Project and one of the country's leading experts on sentencing policy, race, and the criminal justice system. He has directed programs on criminal justice policy reform for thirty years and is the author of some of the most widely cited reports and publications in the field, including *Young Black Men and the Criminal Justice System* and the *Americans Behind Bars* series, comparing international rates of incarceration. His 1995 report on racial disparity and the criminal justice system led the *New York Times* to editorialize that the report "should set off alarm bells from the White House to city halls—and help reverse the notion that we can incarcerate our way out of fundamental social problems." *Race to Incarcerate*, Mauer's groundbreaking book on how sentencing policies led to the explosive expansion of the U.S. prison population, was a semifinalist for the Robert F. Kennedy Book Award in 1999, and was revised in 2006.

Born in Vietnam, **Trinh T. Minh-ha** is a filmmaker, writer, composer, and professor of Rhetoric and Gender and Women's Studies at the University of California, Berkeley. Her work includes ten books, among them, *Elsewhere, Within Here* (2010); *The Digital Film Event* (2005); *Framer Framed* (1992); *When the Moon Waxes Red* (1991); and *Woman, Native Other* (1989). Her work also includes seven feature-length films, which have been honored in numerous retrospectives around the world, including *Night Passage* (2004), *The Fourth Dimension* (2001), and *A Tale of Love* (1996); several collaborative multimedia installations, including *Old Land New Waters* (2007–2008 Third Guangzhou Triennial, 2008), *l'Autre marche* (Musée du Quai Branly, 2006–2009), *The Desert Is Watching* (Kyoto Art Biennial, 2003), and *Nothing But Ways* (Yerba Buena Center for the Arts, 1999). Trinh Minh-ha has been the recipient of numerous awards and grants, including the MIPDoc Trailblazers Award and the AFI National Independent Filmmaker's Maya Deren Award. Her films have been honored in over forty-two retrospectives in the United States, Europe, Asia, and Latin America, and were exhibited at the International Contemporary Art Exhibition, Documenta 11 (2002), in German

Michael Omi teaches Asian American Studies and Comparative Ethnic Studies at the University of California, Berkeley. He is the co-author of *Racial Formation in the United States*, a groundbreaking work that transformed how we understand the social and historical forces that give race its changing meaning over time and place. Professor Omi is a past recipient of UC Berkeley's Distinguished Teaching Award—an honor bestowed on only 232 Berkeley faculty members since the award's inception in 1959.

Since 1995, he has been the co-editor of the book series, *Asian American History and Culture*, at Temple University Press. From 1999 to 2008, he served as a member and as chair of the Daniel E. Koshland Committee for Civic Unity, at the San Francisco Foundation. From 2002 to 2006, he served on the Project Advisory Board on "Race and Human Variation," for the American Anthropological Association, which resulted in the current traveling museum exhibit, Race: Are We So Different? He currently serves as one of the faculty directors of the Center for New Racial Studies, a University of California multi-campus research project, based at UC Santa Barbara.

Nell Irvin Painter is one of the preeminent historians in America today. A graduate of Harvard University, Painter is the Edwards Professor of American History at Princeton University. She is the author of seven books, including her most recent, *The History of White People, Creating Black Americans: African American History and Its Meanings, 1619 to the Present*, and *Southern History Across the Color Line*, as well as countless articles relating to the American South. Painter has been a fellow of the Guggenheim Foundation, the Charles Warren Center for Studies in American History, the Bunting Institute, and the Center for Advanced Study in the Behavioral Sciences at Stanford.

Author, psychiatrist, educator, and respected social critic, Dr. **Alvin F. Poussaint** is one of the nation's top authorities on a wide range of social issues, including multiculturalism, race and ethnic relations, family dynamics, interpersonal communication, and violence prevention initiatives. From 1965 to 1967, Poussaint was Southern Field Director of the Medical Committee for Human Rights in Jackson, Mississippi, providing medical care to civil rights workers and aiding in the desegregation of hospitals and health facilities throughout the South. In 1969, he joined Harvard Medical School, where he is professor of psychiatry and faculty associate dean for student affairs.

Poussaint has written more than 100 articles for both lay and professional publications and is co-author with Dr. James Comer of *Raising Black Children*, co-author with Amy Alexander of *Lay My Burden Down: Suicide and the Mental Health Crisis Among African Americans*, and co-author with Bill Cosby of *Come on People: On the Path from Victims to Victors*.

john a. powell, executive director of the Kirwan Institute for the Study of Race and Ethnicity at The Ohio State University, is an internationally recognized authority in the areas of civil rights, civil liberties, and issues relating to race, ethnicity, poverty, and the law. He also holds the Williams Chair in Civil Rights and Civil Liberties at the Moritz College of Law. He has written extensively on a number of issues, including structural racism/racialization; racial justice and regionalism; concentrated poverty and urban sprawl; opportunity-based housing; voting rights; affirmative action in the United States, South Africa, and Brazil; racial and ethnic identity; spirituality and social justice; and the needs of citizens in a democratic society. Previously, Professor powell founded and directed the Institute on Race and Poverty at the University of Minnesota. He has also served as director of legal services in Miami, Florida, and was national legal director of the American Civil Liberties Union, where he was instrumental in developing educational adequacy theory. He is one of the co-founders of the Poverty and Race Research Action Council and serves on the boards of several national organizations. Powell has taught at numerous law schools, including Harvard and Columbia University. He joined the faculty at The Ohio State University in 2002.

John Telford has long been called a lightning rod for controversy. He retired in 1991 as the deputy superintendent of schools in 98 percent white Rochester, Michigan, where skinheads riddled his house with midnight gunfire for hiring black administrators. After retiring, he became an executive director in the Detroit Public Schools, where he clashed with inept top administrators. He served most recently as the superintendent of the Madison District Schools and was fired for recruiting hundreds of Detroit students against the wishes of white residents. He has written newspaper columns, hosted radio shows, and directed human-rights agencies. A former director of the innovative and controversial Division of Basic Education at Macomb Community College, and a published poet and a former world-ranked sprinter, he also taught at Wayne State and Oakland universities. Wayne State University named Dr. Telford its Distinguished Alumnus of the Year in 2001, for his civil-rights activism.

Lisa Thurau is the founder and executive director of Strategies for Youth, an organization dedicated to improving relations between police and youths, particularly youths of color. Formerly, she served as policy specialist and managing director of the Juvenile Justice Center, of Suffolk Law School.

Johanna Wald is the director of strategic planning at the Charles Hamilton Houston Institute for Race and Justice at Harvard Law School. Previously, she worked at the Civil Rights Project at Harvard, where she served as a writer and editor, senior development officer, and policy analyst. She is also a freelance writer, whose op-eds and articles have appeared in *Salon.com*, *Education Week*, the *Boston Globe*, the Center for American Progress, and the *Nation*.

One of America's most provocative public intellectuals, Professor **Cornel West** has been a champion for racial justice since childhood. His writing, speaking, and teaching weave together the traditions of the black Baptist church, progressive politics, and jazz. the *New York Times* has praised his "ferocious moral vision." Currently the Class of 1943 Professor at Princeton University, Dr. West burst onto the national scene in 1993 with his bestselling book, *Race Matters*, a searing analysis of racism in American democracy. *Race Matters* has become a contemporary classic, selling more than half a million copies to date. In his latest work, *Brother West: Living and Loving Out Loud*, Dr. West traces his transformation from a schoolyard Robin Hood into a progressive cultural icon. Themes include race, leadership, faith, family, philosophy, love, and service. Cornel West has published nineteen other books and has edited thirteen texts. West also offers commentary weekly on *The Tavis Smiley Show*, from Public Radio International. West was an influential force in developing the storyline for the popular *Matrix* movie trilogy and has served as its official spokesperson, as well as played a recurring role in the final two films. Dr. West graduated magna cum laude from Harvard University and has a doctorate from Princeton.

Dr. **James J. Zogby** is founder and president of the Arab American Institute, a Washington, D.C.-based organization that serves as the political and policy research arm of the Arab-American community. He was a cofounder and chairman of the Palestine Human Rights Campaign in the late 1970s. He later co-founded and served as the executive director of the American-Arab Anti-Discrimination Committee. In 1993, following the signing of the Israeli-Palestinian peace accord in Washington, he was asked by Vice President Al Gore to lead Builders for Peace, a private-sector committee to promote U.S. business investment in the West Bank and Gaza. In 1994, with former U.S. congressman Mel Levine, his colleague as co-president of Builders, Zogby led a U.S. delegation to the signing of the Israeli-Palestinian agreement in Cairo.